Praise for *A Great Place to Work For All*

"*A Great Place to Work For All* shines a light on what the best leaders know: great organizations put people first. Bush and his team share their experience and the data to demonstrate that companies that value their employees' interests and priorities are more successful. This book makes it clear that leading companies drive innovation by empowering people at all levels of the organization—helping them thrive, both personally and professionally. Well-written and replete with tips and examples, it's a necessary addition to every business leader's reading list."
—Julie Sweet, CEO, Accenture

"In today's rapidly evolving marketplace, successful companies differentiate themselves by creating an environment where top talent can do the best work of their lives. It begins with a fundamental premise that a leader's job is not to build greatness into people but instead to acknowledge that greatness already exists and to devote energy toward creating an environment where greatness can emerge. *A Great Place to Work For All* defines a compelling blueprint for why this is important and how to transform your own practices into building a world-class environment."
—Brad D. Smith, Chairman and CEO, Intuit

"The most successful companies have a higher purpose and are built on a foundation of trust, growth, innovation, equality, and making the world a better place for all. *A Great Place to Work For All* shares the essential values that every organization should follow to thrive in the future."
—Marc Benioff, CEO, Salesforce

"It's no secret that the world of work has changed drastically, and what defines a great place to work—and a great leader—is the difference between an innovative and mission-driven company and one that remains status quo. *A Great Place to Work For All* builds on a thirty-year legacy of research on thousands of great workplaces and millions of employees to measure the business value of culture, mission, motivation, and leadership. Cultivating human potential for the future requires being intentional in building a caring workplace where employees know they are supported during good and challenging times, the mission remains the heart of the organization, and leaders bring out the best in everyone. This book reveals the opportunities ahead for today's leaders to create a future workplace that delivers results."
—Bernard J. Tyson, Chairman and CEO, Kaiser Permanente

"At Wegmans, we have always believed that we can only achieve our goals by first fulfilling the needs of our people. When we lead with our hearts and live by our values, everything else falls into place, including strong business results. A workplace that fosters caring and respect for one another, at every level of the organization, is key. This is precisely the premise of this book, and by reading it and applying some of the practices, any organization can be transformed."

—Colleen Wegman, President and CEO, Wegmans Food Markets

"When people find opportunity, trust, and camaraderie in the workplace, they proudly drive the success of their organization. The most profitable companies embrace this and welcome the chance to enhance the well-being of all their employees at every level of the organization. *A Great Place to Work For All* gives readers an effective, researched-based look at how to build and maintain an inclusive, high-performing culture—today and beyond. It's sure to become a must-have guide for how to sustain a thriving business that creates value and growth for all stakeholders."

—Arne M. Sorenson, President and CEO, Marriott International, Inc.

"In a world that is increasingly uncertain and that changes constantly, employers must listen and respond to their employees' experiences—in and out of the workplace. Employers have the opportunity to lead with purpose and create an environment of stability to respond to this 'new normal.' I believe that the companies that do this will enjoy lower attrition rates, higher ROI for recruiting efforts, increased creativity and flexibility, engaged managers, and of course, superior work quality. Business leaders must accept that creating great places to work for all is a new business imperative for success, or they risk falling behind."

—Tim Ryan, US Chairman and Senior Partner, PwC

"A company's ability to deliver on its mission is tied directly to the passion, commitment, and resilience of its people. In my experience at Genentech, our capacity to innovate, drive progress, and help people facing serious diseases depended on maintaining a positive and productive environment for all. I believe a critical part of any leader's role is to cultivate a workplace where each person feels connected to a core purpose, valued as an individual, and able to contribute his or her best."

—Ian Clark, former CEO, Genentech

"*A Great Place to Work For All* provides companies a blueprint on how to build a sustainable winning culture. No company can fulfill its potential without attracting and cultivating great people, at all levels of the organization, who know that what they do makes a difference every day. Such a winning culture does not materialize by accident but instead reflects a concerted effort to align values, people programs, and communications in a strategic way."

—**Walter White, President and CEO, Allianz Life Insurance Company of North America**

"In an increasingly volatile and uncertain world, it is vitally important for business leaders to build For All workplaces where people can truly be themselves, be inspired by a compelling purpose, and work hard for the benefit of one another and their customers. For All workplaces have the potential to drive change in society, resetting both our personal and collective expectations ever higher for shared success and opportunity for all."

—**Heather J. Brunner, Chairwoman and CEO, WP Engine**

"Digital disruption is impacting every business around the world, and in these uncertain times companies need to invest more than ever in their people to ensure that they can adapt and innovate. Core values and culture need to be more than a poster on the wall. They need to drive the behavior of your employees. Companies with a strong culture and highly engaged employees will not only survive but thrive and innovate!"

—**Jim P. Kavanaugh, CEO, World Wide Technology**

"*A Great Place to Work For All* skillfully relates how companies that put their people first find the greatest success and that building a culture of trust throughout an organization fuels its growth and performance."

—**Dennis Gilmore, CEO, First American Financial Corporation**

"A true north to be followed by leaders in every industry, *A Great Place to Work For All* compels us to reach for more than financial performance and makes an inspiring argument that only by building an environment of complete trust and a culture of deeper meaning can we create an enduring company with long-lasting growth. We share these beliefs at GoDaddy, and they've been an essential part of our transformation."

—**Blake Irving, former CEO, GoDaddy**

"Let's face the facts. Traditional workplace practices, many designed to simply control and cope with employees, are no longer sufficient and are even being rejected by today's workers who want more. It's time to adopt new constructs that, instead, empower employees to flourish. What's really exciting about *A Great Place to Work For All* is the book's detailed explanations of the specific behaviors required to maximize human potential. This is a must-read for business leaders, HR professionals, line managers, and executives who want to engage our most precious resources: people."

—Dr. Amy Schabacker Dufrane, SPHR, CAE, CEO, HR Certification Institute

A Great Place to Work For All

A Great Place to Work For All

**By Michael C. Bush, CEO
and the Great Place to Work Research Team**

Better for Business.
Better for People.
Better for the World.

BK

Berrett–Koehler Publishers, Inc.
a BK Business book

Berrett-Koehler Publishers, Inc.
1333 Broadway, Suite 1000
Oakland, CA 94612-1921
Tel: (510) 817-2277 | Fax: (510) 817-2278
www.bkconnection.com

ORDERING INFORMATION

Quantity sales. Special discounts are available on quantity purchases by corporations, associations, and others. For details, contact the "Special Sales Department" at the Berrett-Koehler address above.

Individual sales. Berrett-Koehler publications are available through most bookstores. They can also be ordered directly from Berrett-Koehler: Tel: (800) 929-2929; Fax: (802) 864-7626; www.bkconnection.com.

Orders for college textbook/course adoption use. Please contact Berrett-Koehler: Tel: (800) 929-2929; Fax: (802) 864-7626.

Distributed to the U.S. trade and internationally by Penguin Random House Publisher Services.

Berrett-Koehler and the BK logo are registered trademarks of Berrett-Koehler Publishers, Inc.

Great Place to Work®, the Red Box DESIGN®, Accelerated Leadership Performance™, Better People Better Business Better World™, Best Workplaces™, Culture Audit™, For All™, Great Place to Work For All™, GPTW™, Maximizing Human Potential™, Trust Index™, Emprising™, Trust Mindset™, and Innovation By All™ are all trademarks of Great Place to Work Institute Inc.

Accelerated Leadership Performance©, Great Place to Work® Trust Index Employee Survey©, and Great Place to Work® Trust Index©, are copyrights of Great Place to Work Institute Inc.

FORTUNE 100 Best Companies to Work For is a registered trademark of Fortune Inc.

Printed in Canada

Berrett-Koehler books are printed on long-lasting acid-free paper. When it is available, we choose paper that has been manufactured by environmentally responsible processes. These may include using trees grown in sustainable forests, incorporating recycled paper, minimizing chlorine in bleaching, or recycling the energy produced at the paper mill.

Library of Congress Cataloging-in-Publication Data

Names: Bush, Michael C., author. | The Great Place to Work Research Team.

Title: A great place to work for all : better for business, better for people, better for the world / Michael C. Bush, CEO, and The Great Place to Work Research Team.

Description: First Edition. | Oakland : Berrett-Koehler Publishers, 2018.

Identifiers: LCCN 2017042692 | ISBN 9781523095087 (paperback)

Subjects: LCSH: Work environment. | Leadership. | Employee motivation. | BISAC: BUSINESS & ECONOMICS / Workplace Culture. | BUSINESS & ECONOMICS / Leadership. | BUSINESS & ECONOMICS / Motivational.

Classification: LCC HD7261.B967 2018 | DDC 658.3/12—dc23 LC record available at https://lccn.loc.gov/2017042692

FIRST EDITION

23 22 21 20 19 18 | 10 9 8 7 6 5 4 3 2 1

Book producer and text designer: BookMatters, Berkeley, CA; Copyeditor: Lunaea Weatherstone; Proofreader: Janet Reed Blake; Indexer: Leonard Rosenbaum; Illustrations: Majorminor.co

For everyone doing this thing called "work"
—and for those who haven't yet begun

Contents

Foreword

A Better View of Motivation

by Dan Ariely

There is no question that for almost all companies the largest expense, across the board, is employee compensation. Most companies spend the majority of their income to motivate people through salaries and bonuses. But do companies spend this large amount of money in an ideal way or would they be better off spending some of it in other ways?

Some time ago, I sat down for a long discussion with an executive from a very (very) large publicly traded bank. Like many financial firms, his bank gave some people incredible bonuses at the end of their fiscal year, sometimes to the tune of millions of dollars. The executive explained to me the complex and detailed system of equations the bank used to allocate these huge payouts, which had to do with factors like individual contribution, group contribution, the overall function of the bank, and the overall function of the individual in the group. He asked me for my opinion about each one of the parameters, and each of the equations, and we talked about these in detail for two hours.

At the end of the two hours, I asked him to paint for me a picture of how these big bonuses are delivered to people. "Do you give them a check in an envelope?" I asked. "Does the money go directly in their account? Is there some kind of a ceremony? A discussion? Does the boss ask them how they are going to spend the money? Does the boss invite the employee out to celebrate with a glass of wine or beer? Do they shake hands? Is there a hug?"

"Of course not," my interlocutor replied stiffly. "We're XYZ Bank."[1]

"So you're giving people all of this money to motivate them, but you are not taking any non-monetary actions to increase their motivation?" I asked. "What do you think would happen if a boss took out the employee for a celebratory beer? What if the boss gave them some advice about how to spend the money more wisely? How much more motivated would the employee be then?"

"Interesting," he said.

"Maybe we could even quantify the motivational power of a beer," I continued. "For example, what would create stronger long-term motivation and loyalty, a million dollars in an envelope and a handshake, or $950,000 with celebratory beer? What about a million dollars vs. $900,000 with celebratory beer and a hug? The point is, that while your bank is very happy to make up compensation equations and give tremendous amounts of money away, you're not truly exploring the fundamentals of human motivation, you are not investing in human capital, and you are not learning how to get people to care more about what they are doing."

By way of illustration, I described to him an experiment that my colleagues and I had once run at an Intel chip factory. In that experiment, we examined one type of bonus that came in the form of money, another that came in the form of a pizza voucher, and a third that was a compliment from the boss. The results showed that the compliment was the most motivating form of reward. Moreover, while the financial bonus had a short-term positive effect on performance, it had a long-term negative effect on performance, and together the overall long-term effect of the financial bonus was negative. "The main point," I told him, "is that there is a lot more to work than just the opportunity to exchange labor for money."

Like this bank, too many companies fail to understand the complex, intricate topic of motivation and how to optimize it. That's because they perceive themselves as makers of goods like cell phones or pharmaceuticals, or deliverers of services like TV or banking. They don't pay sufficient attention to the parts of the business that don't make it to the balance sheet, or the kinds of things that are not reported to Wall Street. They don't fully realize that companies, and their futures, are largely a sum of their human capital.

Caring for employees, making them feel respected and valued, treating them fairly, giving them opportunities for growth, and taking them out for a celebratory beer once in a while don't have a monetary line item on the P&L sheet, but they can be worth a lot, particularly in the long run. As Great Place to Work's invaluable surveys of millions of employees show very clearly, when employees feel pride in their work, trust in their leaders, and camaraderie with their coworkers, they repay the company with commitment and engagement that also show up on the bottom line. What's more, when companies build a consistently great culture—what Great Place to Work calls a For All culture, the boost is increased even more.

"A Great Place to Work," writes Michael Bush, "is one where employees trust the people they work with, have pride in the work they do, and enjoy the people they work with."

This is not just touchy-feely stuff: the excellent data that Great Place to Work has accrued over time (and that I've used in my own studies on workplace motivation) bears it out. Some of their findings have been surprising. For example, it turns out that people worry less about monetary inequality than they do about the fairness of processes and being treated equally across categories such as gender and race. So it's OK for someone to get a larger bonus than someone else as long as the methodology used to sort out who gets what is understood to be fair and equitable.

There is no question that the engine of growth for any company is the ingenuity of their employees, while the engine of stagnation is employee apathy. This book shines a light on the importance of investments in human capital that go beyond salaries and benefits. In today's workplace, in which work and life are tightly integrated, companies need people to be thinking about work commitments practically around the clock. The only way employees will do that willingly is when they believe that their leaders care for them, that they are treated fairly, and that they're engaged in meaningful work. By investing more in human capital, companies can do much better for all their stakeholders—for shareholders, for the people who work there, and for the world.

Dan Ariely is the James B. Duke Professor of Psychology and Behavioral Economics at Duke University and the author of several books, including *Predictably Irrational, The Upside of Irrationality, The Honest Truth about Dishonesty,* and *Dollars and Sense.*

Introduction

A Great Place to Work For All

What was good enough to be "great" 10 or 20 years ago is not good enough now. To survive and thrive in the future, organizations have to build Great Places to Work For All.

Like other business leaders, John Chambers likes to win.

But his way of winning is different.

We recently spoke with the longtime CEO of tech giant Cisco Systems, and his face lit up when he talked about outlasting rival networking firms and the thrill of outmaneuvering business opponents by thinking ahead.

"The chess game is fun," said Chambers, who stepped down from the CEO post three years ago but remains at Cisco as executive chairman. "I never make the first move on the chessboard until I've already played the game forward and backward."[2]

He plays it well. During Chambers' 20 years as CEO, Cisco's annual revenue soared from $1.2 billion to $47 billion, the company laid the plumbing for the modern Internet, and *Business Insider* named it one of the "Greatest Tech Companies in History."[3]

So, in many ways, Chambers is the quintessential take-charge, no-nonsense, play-to-win business executive. But something sets him apart. Unlike most business leaders of his era, Chambers realized early on that a key to winning as a leader is tapping your people power—that is, creating a great place to work, where people bring their best selves to the organization.

Chambers calls it "culture," or you might call it the queen piece in his chess matches. "While some people view culture as not a key ownership requirement for the CEO, I respectfully disagree," he said. "I think it is the foundation."

Chambers' focus on culture is why Cisco has been a mainstay on the 100 Best Companies to Work For list we publish each year with our partner FORTUNE magazine. Cisco, in fact, is one of the 12 "Legend" companies that earned a place on our list each of the first 20 years we produced it.

At a recent Great Place to Work For All conference, Chambers spoke from the main stage to our "choir"—the community of companies that already get the importance of a great culture. But he had a sermon about the emerging digital economy that shook people up.[4]

The speed of change is accelerating, Chambers said. And that means, more than ever, everyone in the organization counts. Companies won't be able to win if they wait for senior executives to learn about problems and make decisions. Today, there are 17 billion devices connected to the Internet, Chambers said, and that number will explode to 500 billion in 10 years, meaning companies will have to make sense of unprecedented amounts of data. "You're going to have information coming into your company in ways you never imagined before," he said. "Decisions will be made much further down in the organization at a fast pace."

The upshot of his message is agility and success in today's chess matches require getting all your people into the game—making decisions rather than serving as passive pawns.

What John Chambers told our conference audience gets at the heart of this book. What was good enough to be great 10 or 20 years ago is not good enough anymore.

Decades of Studying Greatness

Our organization, Great Place to Work, should know. For more than two decades, we have conducted one of the largest employee surveys in the world, mainly through our research for the many Best Workplaces lists we produce in partnership with business publications spanning the globe. In the United States, we are best known for producing the annual FORTUNE 100 Best Companies to Work For in America and other Best Workplaces lists. However, we create similar lists in more than 50 countries across six continents.

Each year, we survey as many as 4 million employees globally at more than 6,000 companies—firms that collectively employ roughly 10 million people. In the United States alone, we polled nearly 650,000 employees in 2016, obtaining results that reflect the views of about 4.5 million American workers. The companies we survey represent virtually every size and industry.

Over time, this has amounted to a trove of data on what

Great Place to Work Trust Index Employee Survey

One of the World's Largest Employee Surveys

- 3 million+ surveys representing roughly 10 million employees per year
- 58 countries across six continents
- 6,000+ companies per year
- Based on 30 years of data

---

employees experience when their company is a Great Place to Work—and how leaders can build one. We have learned great workplaces are not created through a particular set of benefits, unique to a particular industry, limited to public or private organizations, or the advantages of large or small organizations. Instead, universally, a Great Place to Work is one where employees trust the people they work for, have pride in the work they do, and enjoy the people they work with.

> **"**
> **Our 30 years of research shows a Great Place to Work is one where employees trust the people they work for, have pride in the work they do, and enjoy the people they work with.**
> **"**

When we started this work, our goal was to understand and celebrate what type of work experience was considered "great" by employees. In the process of that analysis, we discovered something even more powerful. The same qualities employees around the world report make a great workplace—trust, pride, and camaraderie—also fuel business performance.

For example, as we will discuss in Chapter 1, the publicly held companies that appear on the FORTUNE 100 Best list have delivered stock market returns two to three times greater than major stock indices. And it doesn't stop there. Relative to their competitors, great workplaces win when it comes to revenue growth, employee retention, productivity, innovation, resilience, agility, customer service, employee engagement, and more. Internationally, we have found the same holds true.

Thanks in large part to our data and the findings of other researchers, leaders over the past 20 years have increasingly recognized that doing well by their people also serves their business.

A New Frontier

But this general formula isn't good enough anymore.

The chess game has changed, and our newest research shows that what it means to be a great workplace has evolved.

> **"**
> **The new frontier in business is about improving results by developing every ounce of human potential.**
> **"**

We have entered a new era, a new frontier in business. This largely uncharted territory is about growing your business and improving results by developing every ounce of human potential within the people who work there. Our economy has evolved through agrarian, industrial, and "knowledge" phases to the point where the essential qualities of human beings—things like passion, creativity, and a willingness to work together—are the most critical. Societal and technological changes are creating new opportunities and challenges for organizations as they seek to attract the best talent and win over customers. Fast-changing competitive landscapes are putting a premium on agility and redefining what it looks like.

More people, of more diverse backgrounds, are speaking up and being heard. The massive millennial generation expects their workplaces to provide meaning, balance, and career development. Millennials also expect the brands they buy to hold the same values and will judge them harshly not just if they fail consumers but if they fail their own employees as well. Female employees, as well as those from different racial and ethnic groups, are also speaking up, sharing injustices faced in the workplace on the social media airwaves, and demanding equality.

All these changes mean companies must clear a higher bar in creating cultures that are welcoming to everyone. Our research, for example, shows that female employees who don't feel they can have honest conversations with leaders have a lower overall workplace experience and are more likely to jump ship. On the flip side, we found that among the often-criticized group of millennial employees, those who experience their company as a great workplace are 20 times more likely to plan a long-term future there than those who do not.

The Best Companies to Work For in the United States have improved for employees over the past two decades, *on average*. But our data shows they are, to a great degree, still wasting human potential. They typically have pockets of people who do not feel fully alive at work and therefore are not contributing their best ideas or bringing their best selves to work.

A New Era for Great Place to Work

We began to focus on the way many great workplaces have been great for some but not all in 2015. That's when I joined Great Place to Work as CEO. I knew employees at many of our Best Workplaces—and knew some of these people were not having a great experience. What's more, as I met with customers they pushed us to innovate our methodology, given the new challenges their businesses were facing.

So we dug into our data. The resulting analysis created a new purpose for us. If we're going to call a company "great," it's got to be great for everybody. It's got to be a Great Place to Work...For All.

A Great Place to Work For All has six components we now measure:

1. Values
2. Innovation
3. Financial Growth
4. Leadership Effectiveness
5. Maximizing Human Potential
6. Trust

The first four items make sense to any leader running an organization. Item 5, Maximizing Human Potential, resulted from a review of our survey data, which showed significant discrepancies in the work experience between executives and those on the front lines. Between men and women. Between different generational cohorts. Between people of different ethnic and racial identities.

So we decided to raise the bar in our model and our methodology to reflect the new For All standard. Central to our new approach is maximizing human potential; we are now assessing how well companies create a consistently positive experience for all employees, no matter who they are or what they do for the organization. We made this shift to reflect the reality of the world today, and to recognize and learn from the inclusive organizations that are setting the pace. Not just for moral reasons but for business reasons. Our most recent research shows companies that rate most highly according to our new For All standard grow revenue three times faster than their less-inclusive rivals.

In other words, while trust fuels business performance at great workplaces, For All accelerates it. In a separate study, we found the organizations scoring highest using our new For All methodology grew their revenue about 10 percent faster over the same period than the companies that scored best according to our old methodology, which simply measured *average* levels of trust, pride, and camaraderie (see Figure 6 on page 28).

> **"**
>
> **In the emerging economy, leaders have to create an outstanding culture for everyone, no matter who they are or what they do for the organization. They have to build Great Places to Work For All.**
>
> **"**

It makes sense that For All organizations race ahead, because now business success relies on developing all your human potential. Every employee matters in an economy that is about connectivity, innovation, and human qualities like passion, character, and collaboration.

The upshot is, in the emerging economy, the Best Workplaces can do better—much better. And they must. They have to work in new ways and with new behaviors to create an outstanding culture for everyone, no matter who they are or what they do for the organization.

The same is true for all organizations. To survive and thrive in the future, organizations have to build Great Places to Work For All.

A New Model

The six elements of a Great Place to Work For All are each important in their own right. They also fit together. Organizations are able to maximize human potential through leadership effectiveness, meaningful values, and a culture where all employees experience high levels of trust. When those pieces are in place, companies benefit from improved innovation and financial growth. In effect, the six elements work together to create a portrait of a Great Place to Work For All (see Figure 1).

It's a thing of beauty. But creating it amounts to a challenge to leaders: to recognize human potential is the name of the new game, fairness is the playbook, and the companies that reach all of their people win. In this new era, it will be critical for CEOs to make sure their workforce and their executive team reflect the world around them. You can't have a For All workplace if you don't have *all* kinds of people there in the first place. In addition, executives who reflect the population are

Figure 1

Portrait of a Great Place to Work For All

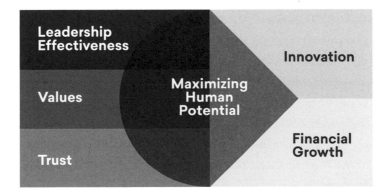

essential for understanding customer needs and for retaining and inspiring employees lower down in the organization. People need to see leaders who look like them to believe they can advance and for them to fundamentally trust their executives.

Apart from reflecting on the makeup of the C-suite—and changing it if necessary—leaders face another major adjustment. Much of the leadership development industry in recent years has told leaders to look within themselves. It's not wrong to focus on strengths and passions, but it's not enough in a world where the pace of business is picking up, diverse perspectives are critical, and everyone wants a say. Today's leaders have to look outward as well—at the business landscape, of course, but also at their employees. They must get objective data on what their people are experiencing, what employees believe is working and not working. Assessment tools today, from us and others, allow for surgical precision in terms of how to improve. Employee survey data, when you measure metrics that actually drive your business and culture, is the "last mile" for making your leaders better and your culture consistently strong.

A Grim Reality, a New Hope

Many workplace cultures today are weak. Grim, even. Around the globe, today's businesses have people who do not feel inspired or heard, who feel strained and stretched and insecure. Many workplaces not only deaden the spirit and overwhelm the mind but kill the body too—in some cases through dangerous work conditions but also through job stress that leads to heart disease and other health problems that shave years from our lives.

Business executives may earn more money and even enjoy their jobs, but many pine for a deeper sense of purpose. They also worry about slow growth, an ever-changing business landscape, and how to get more from their people, many of whom are anxious and disengaged.

But there's hope in Great Places to Work For All.

Our goal in writing this book is to inspire business leaders to wield their power toward greatness: to improve the performance of their businesses, the lives of the people who work there, and the state of the world at large by building Great Places to Work For All. This book is organized into three sections that address these areas and paint the picture of the type of leader who is able to achieve a For All workplace.

66

Leaders who commit to building Great Places to Work For All have the power to repair and strengthen social bonds, improve individual lives, and elevate the human spirit.

99

Part One, "Better for Business," is the heftiest section and provides a business case for why leaders should make building a Great Place to Work For All a top strategic priority. Here, we share anecdotes and evidence illustrating the ways high-trust cultures boost revenue and business success. We also explain how Great Places to Work For All foster more agility, making them critical to business survival in an increasingly fast-paced, hypertransparent, technology-driven landscape. We offer a detailed description of the six elements of a Great

Place to Work For All. And we round out the section by taking a deep dive into our latest data that identifies the specific gaps in experience reported by different demographic groups in the workplace. We show how when these gaps are closed, human potential is maximized and organizations outpace rivals.

Part Two, "Better for People, Better for the World," examines the tremendous impact the workplace has on human beings and on the world at large. Through real examples from great workplaces, we show that when people have a positive experience of work, and are able to bring the best of themselves, they enjoy healthier, more fulfilling lives. In this section, we also take a global view of the workplace as a key lever for building a world defined by shared prosperity, fairness, and individual opportunity. We show how leaders who commit to building Great Places to Work For All have the power to repair and strengthen social bonds, improve individual lives, and elevate the human spirit.

Part Three, "The For All Leadership Call," shifts attention to the For All Leader profile and the next steps leaders can take after reading the book to accelerate leadership performance for themselves and their teams. Here, we share our new research involving 10,000 managers and 75,000 employees, which has allowed us to identify five leader personas: the Unintentional Leader, the Hit-or-Miss Leader, the Transactional Leader, the Good Leader, and the pinnacle For All Leader. We also share the business performance associated with each level and provide data-backed recommendations for "leveling up" as a leader.

A New Mission

We're so convinced that Great Places to Work For All are better for business, better for people, and better for the world that we've updated our mission. It now includes the For All piece: our mission is to build a better world by helping organizations become Great Places to Work For All. And we've set a deadline for achieving it: we want every organization across the globe to be a Great Place to Work For All by 2030.

> **66**
>
> We have a new mission and a deadline for it—we want every organization across the globe to be a Great Place to Work For All by 2030.
>
> **99**

Yes, this is a lofty goal. But we've been here before. When we began exploring the idea of a Great Place to Work three decades ago, the concept was not mainstream. Our first 100 Best list with FORTUNE in 1998 was an oddity. Caring about a great culture was considered outlandish by most business leaders. Today, organizations routinely include a great workplace as a core strategic priority, thanks in part to the impact of our Best Workplace lists and certification programs.

The same thing is happening again. There's a vanguard working to crack this For All concept. The Best Workplaces are moving quickly to become Great Places to Work For All. We hear their curiosity about what For All means and see them nodding in agreement with our new methodology. Soon, workplaces that are great for everyone will be the new baseline expectation for employees, customers, and the broader public. If anything, change may come faster this time around, because we aren't alone in 2018. More and more business leaders around the world are taking courageous, public stances in favor of a For All world.

We hope this book inspires you to join them and us on our mission. You may be the kind of leader who loves to compete and win the chess match. Or maybe you are driven more by the idea of creating a great company for your employees. Or by the goal of making the world a better place.

No matter what spurs you on, the way forward is the same: creating a Great Place to Work For All.

Part One

Better for Business

Chapter 1
More Revenue,
More Profit

**Great Places to Work For All are better for business.
A consistent high-trust culture is quickly becoming
critical for business success.**

To see the way a Great Place to Work For All wins in business,
look at how a For All culture wins on the basketball court.

That is, look at the Golden State Warriors. The professional basketball team of the San Francisco Bay Area has
a motto of "Strength in Numbers," and they live up to it. In
contrast to the conventional style of play that isolates the
most talented players for scoring chances or defensive stops,
the Warriors pass the ball incessantly on offense. And their
defense involves all five players working together as a unit,
constantly helping each other out and switching assignments.

For the 2016–17 season, they ranked as the second-most
stingy defense in the NBA. The Warriors also ranked as the
most efficient offense the past two years. They have finished
first in assists each of the past three years—a sign of the cooperative, unselfish play that leads to easy baskets. These include the many three-point, long-distance shots that earned
Warriors guards Stephen Curry and Klay Thompson the nick-
name "the Splash Brothers."

Overall, the Warriors' success over three seasons is unprecedented. They won 207 games amid just 37 losses—the
best regular-season record in a three-year stretch in NBA

history. The team won the league championship in 2015, came within a hair's breadth of winning it in 2016, and won the title again in 2017.

To be sure, a key to the Warriors' strong performance is the individual talent of their players, including two-time Most Valuable Player Curry as well as all-stars Thompson, Kevin Durant, and Draymond Green. But the players are thriving in a culture that consciously builds trust and a strong, inclusive community. Coach Steve Kerr took the reins of the team in 2014, and one of his first acts was to establish a set of values that ran counter to business as usual in pro basketball. Kerr, a former player and NBA champion himself, declared "competition" to be one of the team's four guiding principles. Nothing shocking there. But here were the three others: joy, mindfulness, and compassion.[5]

In effect, Kerr wanted to bring a human touch to a sport that has at times taken itself too seriously and too often treated players more as machines than people with a love for the game. The compassion piece also signaled a level of caring and vulnerability rarely heard from a leader in any professional arena, let alone athletics.

The values aren't just words on a wall for the Warriors. The team has stood out for team chat threads, group dinners, goofy pranks on each other off the court, and giddy celebrations during games.

Much of the esprit de corps flows from Kerr himself. He has proven to be a leader who respects everyone associated with the team and is willing to diversify his talent pool. For example, Kerr made a key strategy shift in the 2015 finals series based on a recommendation from one of his lowest-ranking coaching assistants. His staff includes a 70-year-old assistant coach—Ron Adams—and a female head of physical performance and sports medicine. And while Kerr is not shy about instructing his players, he is known for hearing them out as well. "Steve is a very good listener and because of that is able to solicit good ideas from his players," Adams says. "They know what they say is going to be listened to and respected."[6]

Sports are always about teamwork, but the Warriors have pushed the concept to a new level. They are reaping the rewards of that push, including in the key area of talent attraction. Crucial to the 2017 title win was adding Durant, a former league Most Valuable Player, who was drawn to the Warriors' camaraderie and winning ways.[7]

Those winning ways are fueled by a culture that consciously brings out the best in everyone.

In effect, the Warriors are a perfect example of how Great Places to Work For All are better for business. Most organizations aren't trying to win basketball games. But the same For All culture found in the Warriors will allow any business to enjoy more revenue and more profit.

Trust Fuels Performance

Central to a For All culture is a high level of trust. Our data and other evidence have demonstrated that high-trust cultures win in business.

For more than 30 years, Great Place to Work has studied and recognized organizations with high-trust cultures, in part through the Best Workplaces lists produced in partnership with FORTUNE magazine. For these companies, a defining feature of being recognized as a great workplace is a high

What Is a High-Trust Culture?

It is a workplace where trust-based relationships are highly valued. In our 30 years of research, we have found that employees experience high levels of trust in the workplace when they

 > Believe leaders are credible (i.e., competent, communicative, honest)

 > Believe they are treated with respect as people and professionals

 > Believe the workplace is fundamentally fair

level of organization-wide trust, as reported by employees. This research, along with findings from various independent research groups, illustrates that high levels of trust pay off. Among the business benefits of high-trust cultures are:

 > Stock market returns two to three times greater than the market average (see Figure 2).

    For more than a decade, an independent investment firm has tracked the stock performance of the publicly traded FORTUNE 100 Best Companies to Work For. In a simulated portfolio that is reset with newly named list companies each year, the research shows Best Companies have a cumulative return nearly three times the benchmark Russell 3000 and Russell 1000 indices.

    A separate, independent study came to similar conclusions. Alex Edmans of the London Business School conducted a complex four-year study that proved a high-trust culture precedes the Best Workplaces' strong stock market performance, and not the other way

Figure 2

High-Trust Cultures
Win in the Stock Market

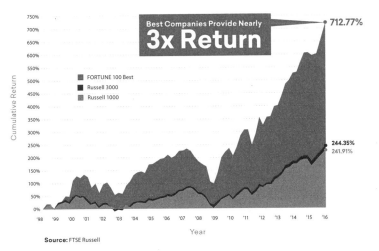

Source: FTSE Russell

around. He also found the 100 Best Companies delivered stock returns that beat their peers by 2 to 3 percent per year over a 26-year period.[8]

> Turnover rates approximately 50 percent lower than industry competitors (see Figure 3).

> Increased levels of innovation, customer and patient satisfaction, employee engagement, organizational agility, and more.

A Great Place to Work study of the hospitals that made the 2016 FORTUNE 100 Best Companies to Work For list found that, on average, these high-trust hospitals have Hospital Consumer Assessment of Healthcare Providers and Systems (HCAHPS) patient satisfaction scores that are significantly higher than the U.S. average

Figure 3

High-Trust Cultures Enjoy Low Turnover

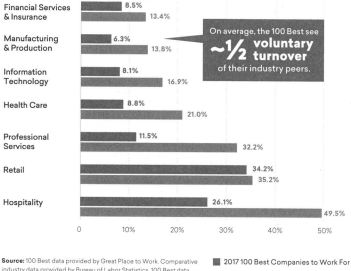

	100 Best	National Industry Average
Financial Services & Insurance	8.5%	13.4%
Manufacturing & Production	6.3%	13.8%
Information Technology	8.1%	16.9%
Health Care	8.8%	21.0%
Professional Services	11.5%	32.2%
Retail	34.2%	35.2%
Hospitality	26.1%	49.5%

On average, the 100 Best see ~1/2 **voluntary turnover** of their industry peers.

Source: 100 Best data provided by Great Place to Work. Comparative industry data provided by Bureau of Labor Statistics. 100 Best data includes full- and part-time turnover; BLS data includes the same in addition to turnover for temporary/contract workers.

■ 2017 100 Best Companies to Work For
■ National Industry Average

for overall hospital rating and whether patients would recommend the hospital (see Figure 4). As patients are the end "customer" in a health care setting, these results demonstrate the positive impact a high-trust culture can have on the overall customer experience.

For All Accelerates Performance

So, high-trust workplaces outpace business rivals. But our latest research shows organizations must clear an even higher bar to reach their full potential.

As great as the 100 Best Companies are, they typically

Figure 4
High-Trust Hospitals
Get Healthier Marks

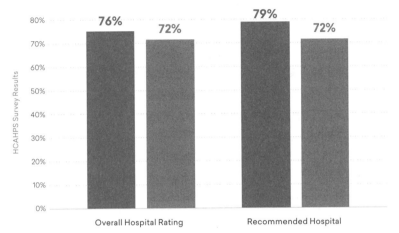

Source: Great Place to Work analysis of HCAHPS Scores

have had significant gaps in the employee experience between groups of people. For example, there are sizeable gaps in the work experience between men and women, salaried workers and non-salaried workers, and executives and individual contributors, to name a few of these differences. These gaps mean not everyone is having a positive experience, which means they are not likely to bring the best of what they have to offer to the organization.

At the same time, we are entering a new frontier in business. This largely uncharted territory is about developing every ounce of human potential, because every employee matters in an economy that is about connectivity, innovation, and human qualities like passion, character, and collaboration.

Societal and technological changes are creating new

opportunities and challenges for organizations in the competition for loyal customers and talented employees. The
millennial generation, in particular, is a highly diverse group
that expects meaning, growth, and balance at work. A reputation for developing employees and for welcoming people from
all backgrounds and walks of life is increasingly crucial to
attracting and retaining the best team possible. In short, the
emerging business climate compels organizations to create an
outstanding culture for everyone.

Our latest research backs the idea that organizations must
create Great Places to Work For All to thrive. For one thing, we
found Great Places to Work For All leave competitors in the
dust. In studying employee surveys from the 2017 100 Best
and the non-winning contender companies, we found the
more consistent an organization is on metrics related to innovation, leadership effectiveness, and trust, the more likely
it is to outperform peers in revenue growth. In particular,
companies in the top quartile on these metrics—which we call
our For All Score—enjoy more than three times the revenue
growth of companies in the bottom quartile (see Figure 5).

We also found Great Places to Work For All grow their
revenue faster than companies that simply show high levels of
trust *on average*.

Up until this past year, we measured the employee experience by examining the overall, average response to our
Trust Index Employee Survey. This "old" approach—which
has been the foundation of our ranking of the FORTUNE 100
Best Companies to Work For list for the past 20 years—didn't
take into account statistically significant gaps that may exist
between demographic groups.

Figure 5

Great Places to Work For All Grow Revenue Faster

Part 1

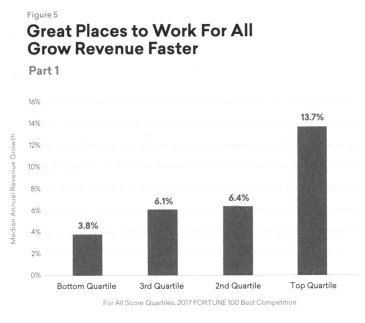

For All Score Quartiles, 2017 FORTUNE 100 Best Competition

Source: Great Place to Work analysis

In 2017, the organizations that ranked highest according to the new For All methodology proved to be a different set of companies than those that ranked highest when using the traditional methodology. And the top tier of these new For All companies grew faster than the best companies determined by our traditional methodology. We found 13.7 percent median annual revenue growth for the top quartile of companies on the For All Score ranking. That compares to 12.5 percent annual revenue growth for the top quartile of companies ranked by our traditional way of gauging the employee experience (see Figure 6).

This follows other evidence from us and others that

Figure 6

Great Places to Work For All Grow Revenue Faster

Part 2

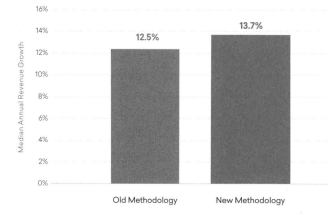

Source: Great Place to Work analysis

inclusive cultures provide more value to shareholders and all stakeholders:

> In a 2015 report, consulting firm McKinsey examined 366 public companies across a range of industries in Canada, Latin America, the United Kingdom, and the United States, and found companies with more diverse workforces perform better financially. Gender-diverse companies were 15 percent more likely to outperform peers with little gender diversity, while ethnically diverse companies were 35 percent more likely to outperform less-diverse peers.[9]

> A 2016 study by the Peterson Institute for International Economics involving nearly 22,000 firms from 91

countries found "the presence of women in corporate leadership positions may improve firm performance" and that "the payoffs of policies that facilitate women rising through the corporate ranks more broadly could be significant."[10]

» Our own research in producing the 2016 Best Workplaces for Diversity list showed that the most inclusive workplaces experienced average annual revenue gains 24 percent higher than their peer companies certified by Great Place to Work.

Our study suggested that just hiring a demographically diverse workforce will not by itself boost results. Simply increasing headcount diversity did not show a strong connection to revenue growth. Instead, our data showed that employees' experience of genuine workplace inclusion—as seen by high, consistent survey scores in areas such as fair treatment and a caring environment—is a better predictor of revenue growth than diversity alone.[11]

Leading companies, including many FORTUNE 100 Best Companies, are on the path to For All workplaces. They are working to close the gaps in the employee experience. And they are seeing payoffs.

Take software giant Salesforce, a perennial 100 Best Company. CEO Marc Benioff and his team invested $3 million in 2015 to address a gender pay gap at the company. The move, along with a host of other equality efforts, has reaped rewards. Salesforce is becoming a beacon for talented women in technology, and it's enjoying the fruits of a more fully engaged workforce. The percentage of women employees who say they want to work at Salesforce for a long time jumped from 85 percent in 2014 to 93 percent in 2016. And 92 percent of female employees in 2016 said people look forward to coming to work at Salesforce, up from 85 percent in 2014.

Salesforce has not rested on its laurels on the gender pay issue. It conducted a similar pay equity study in 2017, investing $3 million more to close compensation gaps. Perhaps not surprisingly, the company has been growing faster than its rivals, and it dominates the customer relationship management software market.[12,13]

But the Golden State Warriors may be the winningest of them all these days—and not just on the court. With its "Strength in Numbers" culture as a foundation, the franchise has been raking in business rewards as well. The value of the team rose an NBA-high 37 percent to $2.6 billion in 2017, leapfrogging from sixth place to third place in the league.

With their season ticket renewal rate at 99.5 percent, the Warriors felt confident enough in 2017 to raise season ticket prices by 15 to 25 percent. And the organization landed a $300 million deal with Chase to name the Warriors' new stadium—a record price for a U.S. arena.[14]

Warriors co-owner Joe Lacob caught some flak for boasting in a 2016 *New York Times* profile that the organization, with its "Silicon Valley precepts" such as open communication and collaborative decision making, is superior to its peers. "We're light-years ahead of probably every other team in structure, in planning, in how we're going to go about things," Lacob told the *Times*.[15] Lacob may be guilty of bravado, but there's little arguing with the way he and his partners have seen their investment blossom. They bought the team for $450 million in 2010, meaning their ROI as of 2017 was a gain of nearly 500 percent.

The Warriors culture is where businesses must go as well. The business case for a Great Place to Work For All isn't merely a two-point slam dunk. It's better. It's a three-point splash.

Chapter 2

A New Business Frontier

Social and technology changes require a new way of doing business.

The rules of the road in business have changed. Just ask Uber.

In a few short years, the ride-sharing service both transformed the transportation industry and found itself crashing against new standards related to leadership, transparency, and fairness.

With its phone-based app for arranging car trips, Uber pioneered a new, cheaper, more convenient way of getting around. It jump-started the "gig economy" by tapping independent contractors rather than traditional employees and quickly became a global force. Eight years into its existence, Uber's revenue in 2016 had raced to $6.5 billion and it was valued at $70 billion—$15 billion more than General Motors.[16]

But its brash CEO Travis Kalanick also steered into one accident after another. In January 2017, Kalanick and the company were slammed for allegedly seeking to profit when taxi drivers protested the Trump administration's refugee ban. Fueled by a #DeleteUber campaign on Twitter, roughly 500,000 users reportedly asked to delete their Uber accounts in the wake of that incident.[17]

The negative publicity continued in February 2017. Former Uber engineer Susan Fowler published a blog post claiming a culture of sexism at the company—including her charge that Uber refused to punish her manager after he made sexual advances, in part because he was a "high performer."[18] There were legal troubles as well, including a U.S. Justice Department probe.[19] Kalanick's reputation was further bruised by a video of him losing his temper with an Uber driver over fare policy.[20] Several executives departed amid all the troubles.[21]

Along with the scandals came a financial warning sign: Uber was burning through cash at an astounding rate. It posted net losses that rose to nearly $1 billion in the last quarter of 2016—an amount that may have been the largest quarterly deficit in business history.[22] Meanwhile, rival Lyft added more than 50 cities to its operations, and other companies were considering entering the ride-share market.[23]

Uber tried to course correct in early 2017. The company put a plan in place to fix its culture, and fired 20 employees in June because of harassment, discrimination, and inappropriate behavior.[24] And Kalanick pledged to get leadership coaching in the wake of his altercation with the driver.[25] But it wasn't enough to prevent investors from pushing him out of the driver's seat.[26] Kalanick stepped down as CEO on June 21, remaining on the company's board of directors.[27]

What a Difference 20 Years Make

Whether Uber's culture flaws, scandals, and executive shake-up amounted to minor potholes or an insurmountable roadblock remained to be seen as of mid-2017. But the company's valuation undoubtedly backtracked amid all the trouble. And the very fact that it careened so wildly speaks to the way the business world has changed in the past two decades.

Think back 20 years, and one can imagine Uber zooming smoothly past most or all of its recent troubles. Back then, consumers were less concerned with the ethics and politics of the companies in their lives. There were no social media networks where a company protest could catch fire so quickly. The Internet wasn't yet a platform for giving any unhappy employee a forum to publish their views to the world. Nor had a culture of self-expression emerged—one that is intertwined with the millennial generation's demand for a meaningful, positive purpose and a growing willingness on the part of people to leave a job if the company doesn't match their values.

Put simply, dramatic societal and technological changes are creating new challenges for organizations as they seek to attract the best talent as well as win over customers. The days of unreformed "bad-boy" CEOs are numbered. Rapidly changing competitive landscapes are putting a premium on agility and redefining what it looks like. The need for decentralized decision making increases the importance of getting the best from everyone. Also making people issues more crucial is a shift to an economy where essential human qualities such as passion, collaboration, and creativity are vital to business success.

In effect, we have entered a new business frontier. This chapter maps how the landscape has shifted thanks to social and technology changes. It explains why business must change to succeed, and shows that what was good enough to be "great" 10 or 20 years ago is not good enough now.

Social Changes

Businesses today are operating in a society that expects more out of companies, that is more demographically diverse, and whose members aren't afraid of speaking up and out. In effect, people are holding the companies in their lives to a higher standard as consumers, investors, and employees.

In the wake of the Great Recession of 2008, consumers now seek "value and values," according to research by journalist Michael D'Antonio and John Gerzema, the president of Brand Asset Consulting for global advertising firm Young & Rubicam. D'Antonio and Gerzema found that more than 71 percent of Americans are part of a "spend shift," in which consumers are actively aligning their spending with their values. This shift cuts across demographic groups and is rewarding companies that demonstrate transparency, authenticity, and kindness in their operations.[28]

Meanwhile, American businesses face an increasingly diverse marketplace. Whites made up 80 to 90 percent of the U.S. population from 1790 to 1980. The year 2011 marked the first "majority-minority" birth cohort, in which the majority of U.S. babies were nonwhite minorities.[29]

The demographic changes come with cultural divides. Many baby boomers (those born from 1946 to 1964) and seniors (those born earlier still) resist the changing racial makeup of the country, while the millennial generation (those born from 1981 to 2004) is more inclusive. One study found just 36 percent of baby boomers thought more people of different races marrying each other was a change for the better, compared to 60 percent of millennials who applauded the trend.[30]

The millennial generation is one businesses have to pay close attention to, as both consumers and workers. Millennials surpassed their Generation X elders (born from 1965 to 2000) as the largest cohort in the U.S. workforce in 2015.[31]

That year, there were an estimated 53.5 million millennials at work, or about one-third of U.S. workers.

As employees, millennials prioritize meaning, balance, and job stability. A recent survey of 81,100 U.S. undergraduates found young people ranked an inspiring purpose as the most desired characteristic in an employer, with other top priorities being job security, work–life balance, and working for a firm with fewer than 1,000 employees.[32] Millennials also expect a more personalized, development-oriented, participatory, collaborative, and transparent workplace, other research shows.[33]

That's not to say that desires like purpose and cooperation are absent in people of other generations. After all, the "Greatest Generation" of Americans had the courage to defeat the Nazis in World War II, rebuild Europe, and put a man on the moon. Baby boomers and Generation Xers have had the vision and persistence to launch companies that have reshaped the way we live: firms like Microsoft, Genentech, Whole Foods Market, Apple, and Google, to name a few.

It could be that millennials have such lofty standards for work in part because they happen to have been raised during the economic boom of the 1990s. And many have entered the workforce during the U.S. recovery that began in 2009. In any event, this generation does stand out from others when it comes to the traditional climb up the corporate ladder. Our research, for example, discovered that baby boomers or Gen Xers generally have a more positive workplace experience the higher the job level they attain. Millennial executives, though, have a less positive experience than millennials in more junior

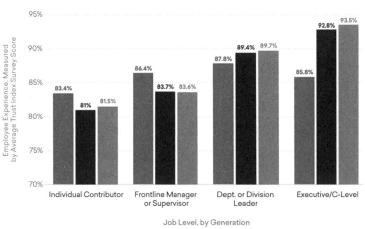

Figure 7

Millennials: A Dip at the Top

Millennial leaders see their work experience drop when they reach the executive level

- Millennials
- Gen Xers
- Baby Boomers

Employee Experience, Measured by Average Trust Index Survey Score

95%

93.5%
92.8%

90%
89.4% 89.7%
87.8%

86.4%
85.8%
85%
83.4%
83.7% 83.6%
81% 81.5%

80%

75%

70%

Individual Contributor | Frontline Manager or Supervisor | Dept. or Division Leader | Executive/C-Level

Job Level, by Generation

Source: Great Place to Work analysis

management roles (see Figure 7). This could be a result of a clash between the demands of C-suite positions and millennials' yearning for a rich life outside of work.

What's more, millennials are not afraid to seek employment elsewhere if their expectations are not met. Our research on different generations in the workforce found fewer than 5 percent of millennials who do not experience a great workplace plan a long-term future at their companies. That compares to 7 percent of Gen Xers and 11 percent of baby boomers who intend to stay at their companies despite not considering it a great workplace.

On the other hand, our data dispelled a commonly held

Figure 8
Trust Drives
Millennial Retention

■ Often/Almost Always a
  Great Place to Work

■ Often/Almost Always NOT a
  Great Place to Work

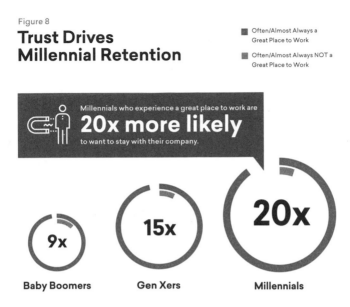

Millennials who experience a great place to work are **20x more likely** to want to stay with their company.

9x — Baby Boomers

15x — Gen Xers

20x — Millennials

myth: that millennials are inveterate job hoppers. We discovered that when young people are at a great workplace, they are nearly as likely as their peers in older generations to want to remain at their companies. Fully 90 percent of millennials who feel they are at a great workplace want to stay there for a long time. In other words, a great workplace makes a 20× improvement when it comes to retention (see Figure 8).

Millennials also tend to voice their opinions and concerns publicly, in company forums, on Facebook, and in blogs. Former Uber employee Susan Fowler, who graduated from the University of Pennsylvania with a bachelor's degree in 2014, is a case in point. Not only did Fowler quit Uber for another firm after just over a year, but she documented her experience for the world to see. Her account not only painted the company as negligent and deceptive regarding her sexual harassment claim but described a back-stabbing, chaotic culture in which a manager allegedly bragged about withholding "business-critical" information from one executive in order to curry favor with another.[34]

Fowler's blog, in effect, was the last straw for Kalanick's reign at Uber. She painted the company as the last place millennials seeking an inspiring, cooperative, transparent culture would want to join or do business with. And given the increasingly important role millennials are playing in the workforce and as consumers, no company can afford to leave this generation behind.

Technology Changes

Susan Fowler's willingness and ability to blog about her Uber experience is directly linked to her coming of age in a world with technologies for widely shared self-expression. Internet blog platforms, social media sites, and related transparency tools are among the technology changes raising the bar for businesses. Other technological developments now facing companies include:

- Increased automation, which paradoxically is putting a premium on the deeply human characteristics of employees
- Big data and the need for analytical chops and a learning mindset
- Heightened digital connectivity, which is accelerating the pace of change and pressuring companies to decentralize decisions

Transparency Tools

Susan Fowler is far from alone in sharing her thoughts online. Overall, 69 percent of the public uses some type of social media platform, such as Facebook, Instagram, or Twitter. That's up from about 50 percent in 2011 and just 5 percent in 2005.[35] Combine that mass usage with people's inclination to discuss work along with the rest of their lives online, as well as the ubiquity of cameras, and nearly everything that takes place in or at a company is at risk of being exposed.

Consider what happened when a passenger was dragged off a United Airlines flight by police officers in early 2017 when he refused to give up his seat. A number of passengers recorded the incident on their phones and posted video on social media. The video quickly went viral and was picked up by major news organizations. In an earlier era, before smartphones and social media, the incident might have been a small news item if it was noticed at all. Instead, the episode turned into a public relations nightmare for United. The day after the incident, United's stock fell about 2.8 percent, wiping out about $600 million in market capitalization.[36]

Increased Automation, More Humanity

Apart from the rise of technologies that effectively disrobe companies, the ongoing march of computing and automation are pressuring organizations to up their game in different ways. Much of the debate in recent years about the "rise of the robots" has been about the way they are reducing the number of jobs in America.[37] That's an important discussion for society overall. But a more immediate impact of automation on companies is counterintuitive: pressure to bring out the least-robotic qualities of the workforce.

In effect, our economy has evolved through agrarian, industrial, and knowledge phases to the point where the essential qualities of human beings are the most critical. Author Dov Seidman uses the term "human economy" to capture this transition.[38] He notes that analytic skills and knowledge—chief traits of what have been called "knowledge workers"—are not advantages in an era of increasingly intelligent machines. Yet people, he writes,

> will still bring to their work essential traits that can't be and won't be programmed into software, like creativity, passion, character, and collaborative spirit—their humanity, in other words. The ability to leverage these strengths will be the source of one organization's superiority over another.

You can see this humanization of work in the shift away from customer service scripts in recent years. Leading hospitality companies, such as Hyatt, have abandoned the robotic responses to customer interactions that had been intended to optimize service levels. Instead, employees from front-desk agents to food service workers are encouraged to have authentic encounters with guests. A few years ago at our annual conference, Hyatt's executive vice president Robert W. K. Webb told a striking story along these lines.[39] A room service worker took a meal to a couple staying at a San Francisco Hyatt and struck up a conversation with them. He learned that they were staying in their room because the wife, in remission from cancer, was too tired to go out on the town that evening. The Hyatt worker, named Andy, also learned that he and the wife shared a love of music, and he began singing Frank Sinatra songs. The couple appreciated his crooning so much that they called for encores, hugged him as he departed, and invited him back the next night. He obliged—this time with Tony Bennett numbers.

The husband wrote Hyatt a letter in gratitude for these surprising serenades. Webb quoted the letter at our event: "The last thing that we were looking for was an experience with room service when we went to San Francisco. But it turned out to be the highlight." The key to this lasting impression was that Hyatt has freed its employees to respond to guests with empathy, creativity, and passion. "Andy was himself," Webb said. "It was magical for them in the moment."

This shift in emphasis from "hired hands" to "hired heads" to "hired hearts," as Seidman puts it, has important consequences for the way businesses manage people. The deadening, disheartening workplaces that most people experience will face an ever-larger penalty. The companies that thrive in the human economy will be the ones that make people feel alive, where workers feel they can bring their full selves, where people reach their full potential as human beings.

Big Data

So technology is pushing companies to make more-humane workplaces. But that's not to say tech shrewdness is not important. On the contrary, firms have to be smart about using computing power to gain insights about all aspects of their business. "Big data" will only become a bigger deal in making savvy decisions about products, pricing, marketing, and people management. For example, assessing data about how employees experience the workplace under different leaders is crucial to making adjustments and optimizing performance.

In general, the need to make data-driven decisions means business leaders will need a willingness to learn—that is, a measure of vulnerability, an open mind willing to forego intuition when the numbers show otherwise.

Digitization

A final technology change forcing companies to do business differently is ever-increasing digital connectivity. Even as growth in global trade has flattened, cross-border data flows have grown by a factor of 45 over the past decade, according to McKinsey Global Institute researchers.[40] Those data exchanges are projected to increase another ninefold by 2020. These digital connections contribute to a faster pace of business, where innovations happen rapidly.[41]

Hyperconnectivity also leads to greater uncertainty. "The competitive landscape is growing more unpredictable as digital platforms such as Amazon, Alibaba, and eBay are empowering companies of any size, from anywhere on Earth, to roll out products quickly and deliver them to new markets," the McKinsey researchers wrote in a 2016 *Harvard Business Review* article.[42]

A New Kind of Agility

A faster pace of business is pushing organizations to be more agile. But the combination of technology and social changes described above is redefining what effective agility looks like. Decades ago, senior executives could survey the business landscape, issue a command about how the organization would change direction, and expect to control the execution of that command.

That old-school command-and-control model breaks down, though, when the time it takes to collect information for a central decision maker can mean missed opportunities. As noted in the introduction, John Chambers, executive chairman of computer networking giant Cisco, deems the traditional, top-down mode of leading obsolete. "Creating an entrepreneurial culture that empowers every employee—from interns to engineers—to create the next big thing is essential to survival," Chambers told us.

Like the shift to "hired hearts," the move to decentralized decision making and what some call a "sense and response" form of leading also makes people management more important. More employees become pivotal to the company's success. If they aren't bringing their best, the company pays a steeper price.

What's more, agility takes a new shape when employees are less willing to be treated as passive cogs in a machine. As discussed above, people today want a sense of purpose at work and to be included in the conversation about where the company is heading. And as changes come faster, the entire organization—everyone in the workforce—needs to be resilient and adaptable in the face of rapid shifts in strategy.

A new model of agility is emerging. Leaders' traditional inclination to hunker down and coil in before springing is less effective. Instead, leaders increasingly must reach out and gather up everyone to manage change.

A good example of this involve-everyone agility can be seen at AT&T. Consider the way the communications giant has pivoted quickly in recent years. For one thing, the company has made radical changes in how it runs its massive network—

handling capacity and services through software rather than hardware. In 2015, AT&T became one of the world's largest providers of pay TV, with the acquisition of DIRECTV. Then in 2016, AT&T and its CEO Randall Stephenson took another bold step to become a major content player with a bid to buy TimeWarner.

As a result of such moves, what was once strictly a telecom company is now a major player in technology, media, and telecommunications. And this puts entirely new demands on its more than 260,000 employees, many of whom started in the landline phone business.

For obvious reasons, the nature of work is changing at AT&T. Soon, some 100,000 positions will require much different technical skills. Stephenson sees this as "the biggest logistical challenge we've ever tackled." But AT&T isn't going to solve the problem by simply letting go of employees who lack cutting-edge capabilities. And it isn't focusing its investments just on "high-potentials."

Instead, Stephenson and AT&T are working to bring all their people forward into the future. The company is inviting them to equip themselves for a digital future, at the company's expense but on their own time. Partnering with educators and investing heavily in new curricula, AT&T aims to keep investing in workforce upskilling for the foreseeable future.

This isn't purely a be-nice-to-workers move on Stephenson's part. As he mentioned at our 2017 Great Place to Work For All conference, retraining existing AT&T employees for the jobs of the future makes the most business sense. "You could not just go out and replace 100,000 people," he said.

"Even if you were a heartless S.O.B., you could not make it happen. The reality was, we were going to have to come at this from the bottom up—build a plan for how you reskill and retool 100,000 people."

AT&T's strategy speaks to a new way of thinking about change and agility. It's about developing and tapping everyone's full human potential. Not only during static times—which are increasingly rare—but during times of tremendous change as well.

New Gig, Old Gig

We've discussed social and technological changes that have dramatically altered the business landscape and transformed organizational agility itself. There's another shift that bears mentioning, an oft-cited change in the business world that isn't as radical as it is sometimes portrayed: the gig economy. The rise of contract work arrangements, in which companies move away from traditional employer–employee relations, does change the workplace landscape significantly. It offers organizations greater financial flexibility even as it raises important societal questions about workers' financial stability and well-being.

But what's sometimes overlooked in conversations about the move to more contract work is that the key, fundamental relationship between organizations and workers doesn't change. People are people. Contractors are drawn to companies they trust, just as employees are. Organizations still need to show contractors credibility, respect, and fairness to attract the best talent and get the most out of their gig workers. You might say that companies should give contractors an "arms-length embrace" to succeed with this growing practice.[43] If they don't show a measure of love to contractors, don't treat them as partners more than transactional entities, organizations will stumble.

Uber, the poster child for the gig economy, learned this lesson the hard way in 2017. Consider the incident in which Travis Kalanick was recorded arguing with an Uber driver. The driver, Fawzi Kamel, told Kalanick that a fare decrease for Uber's high-end "black" cars was unwise and hurt him financially. He says he lost $97,000 and went bankrupt because of Uber's move. "People are not trusting you anymore," he said.

Kalanick didn't try to rebuild Kamel's trust in the exchange. Instead, he offered this retort: "Some people don't like to take responsibility for their own s***. They blame everything in their life on somebody else."

In this case, though, Kamel forced Kalanick to take responsibility for his own "s***." Kamel sent a copy of his dashboard video recording to news outlet Bloomberg. That move turned what would have been a minor annoyance to Kalanick 20 years ago into yet another public relations headache. The incident prompted Kalanick to send a remorseful email to Uber's entire staff. "To say that I am ashamed is an extreme understatement," Kalanick wrote.[44]

Several months later, Kalanick was out as CEO, and the company was working to restore trust with its people and with the public. Whether Uber would succeed remained to be seen. But the company's series of high-profile accidents showed that the economic landscape has transformed over the past two decades. Fundamental changes in society and continued technological advances have created a new set of challenges and opportunities, and a new way of managing change itself.

What was good enough to be great is different today.

It's a new business frontier.

Chapter 3

How to Succeed in the New Business Frontier

The key is maximizing human potential, through leadership effectiveness, values, and trust. Get those right, and you will see innovation and financial growth.

We just covered the new landscape facing organizations. Thanks to social and technology changes, the bar has been raised—what was good enough to be great 20 years ago doesn't cut it today.

Some business basics remain as true today as they have for decades. A successful company must have a sound business model, a smart strategy, and savvy financial management. But these fundamentals of a business school education are no longer sufficient. Leaders' path to success is quickly evolving. Changes happen faster, information moves rapidly with more transparency than ever before, and technology gives any customer or employee the power to be heard worldwide in an instant. These are the unique challenges of our times. And the best leaders are responding.

So what's needed to succeed in the new business frontier? The key is maximizing human potential, accomplished through leadership effectiveness, values, and trust. Get those pieces right, and you will see innovation and financial growth.

Together, those six elements make up the portrait of a Great Place to Work For All (see Figure 9). This chapter details

Figure 9
Portrait of a Great Place to Work For All

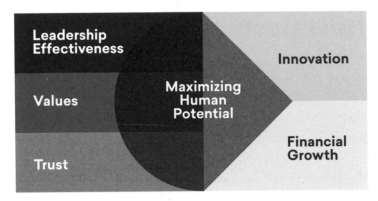

what each means, how they address today's business challenges, and how they fit together.

Lasting success today requires more than many leaders expect. It requires more than we ourselves once thought.

Maximizing Human Potential

Maximizing human potential is central to a Great Place to Work For All. It is pivotal to your success as a leader and a business.

What do we mean by this phrase? Let's start with the "human potential" piece. We mean bringing out the best in your people. Enabling them to reach their potential as human beings—to be as creative, knowledgeable, and productive as possible. This means they are reaching heights they may not have thought possible in terms of projects they undertake, skills they develop, inspiration they feel. Work is not a deadening place or one that is stressful to the point of being debilitating. It is a place where people come alive, where they get in "the flow." Where, in the framework of psychologist Abraham Maslow, they can "self-actualize."[45]

The business case for this is twofold. Being a workplace known for helping people develop into their best selves is becoming critical in terms of attracting talent. Millennials and job seekers of other generations are looking for organizations where they can grow personally and professionally. Beyond talent attraction, a human potential–oriented workplace also is vital in terms of boosting business results. In an economy requiring decentralized agility, constant innovation, and authentic encounters with customers, organizations need a workforce of employees bringing their best.

All employees. An organization where some employees are not bringing their best is leaving money on the table. This is where the "maximizing" piece comes in. If you are not maximizing the human potential in your organization—getting the most from everyone—you cannot realize the full potential of your business. And that spells trouble over time, as competitors are working to realize the full potential of *their* businesses.

Think of it as a ship. When you don't get the most from everyone, you have leaks. Leaks where value, where potential revenue and profit, slip away. Benjamin Franklin once wrote, "Beware of little expenses, a small leak will sink a great ship."

What causes those leaks? Gaps in the workplace experience—that is, people who don't experience as great a workplace as others. Engineers having a different experience than non-engineers. Women who don't have the same access to leaders or opportunities to advance. Frontline workers feeling less purpose and less control over their jobs compared to executives. When these groups have a less-than-great experience at work, they do not reach their full potential. Maslow had it right with his "hierarchy of needs"—to self-actualize, to bring your best, more basic needs must be met. Needs such as a sense that you make a difference, that you belong, that you have a measure of job security. In our 30 years of research in the workplace, we've found these needs boil down to relationships of trust, pride, and camaraderie.

Today, it's common for some employees not to have such needs met as well as other employees. Gaps in workplace experience are commonplace. We find them even at the Best Workplaces. In many cases, these gaps have origins in our broader culture and history, in legacies of discrimination and bias as a country and a species. The gaps may not be caused by today's businesses, but businesses that want to thrive will work to close them.

It may sound daunting, but you can frame the challenge as merely doing for everyone what you are doing for your employees who are thriving most. As lifting all your people up to the standard you've already set for some. When organizations close the gaps, they advance—rapidly. As mentioned earlier in the book, and as we'll explore below and in greater detail in Chapter 4, companies with a more consistently great workplace grow faster. They also outperform rivals in the stock market.

Organizations that maximize human potential are like sleek speedboats. They zip ahead of rivals that are taking on water because of leaky gaps in their workplace experience. Propelled by people-power engines firing on all cylinders, Great Places to Work For All are winning. And leading them is thrilling.

Leadership Effectiveness

In order to maximize human potential, you must have effective leadership.

Effective leadership at a Great Place to Work For All involves toggling back and forth between two major ways of using the brain. Neuroscience has demonstrated the existence of a social cognitive system—the aspects of the brain that allow us to connect as humans and to cultivate meaning for our teams—and a more analytic, "task-positive" network—the portions of the brain that allow us to assess the market and set high-level strategy.[46] These two systems tend to inhibit each other, which means MBA programs that focus almost exclusively on quantitative skills like finance and operations can leave graduates deficient in people skills. Great Place to Work For All executive teams constantly cycle back and forth between these brain systems.

This cycle plays out across four key elements of leadership at a Great Place to Work For All. First, leaders are able to connect on a human, emotional level with employees, no matter who they are or what they do in the organization. They forge meaningful, respectful, caring relationships at work and do so in a fundamentally fair way. Fairness in relationships is particularly vital. It means being aware of implicit biases we all have as human beings. It also requires leaders to be mindful of "stereotype threat"—the way members of minority groups can feel anxious about confirming a stereotype, like "women perform poorly in math."[47]

This is not to say the C-suite team at a 100,000-person company has to get to know every employee on a first-name basis. But all their interactions should reflect humility, acknowledge the dignity of every employee, and demonstrate the organization's values.

There is, however, one group of people with whom senior-most leaders should have strong ties: all the members of the executive team itself. This is the second key element. Executive teams—usually 6 to 12 people in size—must establish high levels of interpersonal trust and successful collaboration. CEOs must surround themselves with people they see as highly credible, consistently respectful, and fair to everyone they meet. The CEO must be seen in an identical way. High-trust, highly functioning executive teams are important in part for effective strategy and execution, but also to serve as a role model for how all teams throughout the organization should interact and perform. Each member of that senior-most team ought to duplicate its culture in their team of direct-reports, those direct-reports cascade the culture to their teams, and so on.

The notion of a positive culture cascading down from the top relates to the third key element of leadership effectiveness: forging and communicating a coherent strategy at every level of the organization. Leaders at the top must explain the company's overall vision in clear and compelling language, and make sure that every business unit understands how it fits into the big picture. Especially when organizations are pushing decision making down to lower levels of the business, a lucid, logical, overarching plan is vital. Otherwise, chaos reigns and ruins employee empowerment efforts.

It's a tricky balance. But when the executive team succeeds in conveying its strategy to lower-level managers and fosters a feeling of purpose, performance takes off. Consider the results of a recent study by researchers at Harvard, Columbia, and New York University on a set of our Best Workplaces. They found when middle managers in publicly traded companies had a strong sense of purpose combined with clarity about management expectations, the firms had superior stock market performance.[48]

The fourth key aspect of effective leadership is a senior leadership team that reflects the demographics of the organization and the wider community. This is critical in part because diverse perspectives generate better decisions.[49] It also is vital because it builds credibility and hope in employees lower down in the organization; when people look up and see others like them in leadership roles, it convinces them they can advance and inspires them to give their all. Ideally, leadership diversity also cascades throughout the organization so that every leader looks to build a diverse team, and you find people from a range of backgrounds at every level of leadership.

When executive teams perform well in these ways, the payoff is big. We created an Executive Effectiveness index that measures how employees view senior leaders on matters such as strategic clarity, even-handedness, and authenticity in their relationships. We found the Great Place to Work–Certified companies with the highest scores on this index grew revenue three times faster than the companies with the lowest scores on the index (see Figure 10).

In short, effective leadership means connecting with your

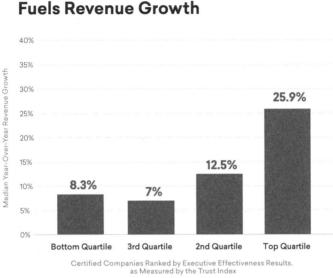

Figure 10

Executive Effectiveness Fuels Revenue Growth

Certified Companies Ranked by Executive Effectiveness Results, as Measured by the Trust Index

Source: Great Place to Work analysis

employees and teams on a strategic and personal level, unlocking the full potential of your people and your organization.

Values

Values aren't a new business topic. But what's old is new again—or important in new ways when it comes to maximizing human potential and succeeding today.

When we talk about values at a Great Place to Work For All, we're not talking about mere slogans on the wall or on the hiring page of your company website. We're talking about principles that guide the day-to-day way people work together at your company. Smart companies today ensure those values and behaviors support their strategy.

Values also are what leaders use to make decisions that cannot be made using spreadsheets and data analysis alone. They are the bedrock principles that guide executives' choices in complex, difficult matters. Matters like hiring, firing, geographic expansions, doing more for customers, and mergers. Values, for example, are central to whether technology giant Cisco pulls the trigger on acquisitions. Many mergers and acquisitions fail, often because of problems blending corporate cultures. But Cisco has a solid track record of effectively making close to 200 acquisitions, in large part by paying close attention to the values and culture of potential targets. "If their culture is dramatically different, we don't touch it," explains executive chairman John Chambers. One time, an acquisition target refused to own up to a stock-options back-dating problem. "If they'd just told me, I would have taken it straight to the government and fixed it. But because they didn't tell us, when we found out, we walked away from the deal," Chambers says.

Values also come to the fore when leaders are faced with what you might call For All decisions. In other words, with how much they are committed to standing up for an organization and a society where everyone is valued. A good example is the way AT&T CEO Randall Stephenson backed the controversial Black Lives Matter movement amid racial tension in 2016. His comments on the topic at an internal meeting were video-recorded—unbeknownst to him—and posted on social media, where they quickly went viral. Among AT&T's values are "care about each other—inside and outside of work" and "do the right thing."[50] In his remarks, Stephenson said his support for Black Lives Matter stemmed from a personal epiphany:

he had learned only recently that his best friend, a black physician, had experienced discrimination on many occasions throughout his life. It struck Stephenson that if he and his close friend hadn't managed to discuss these problems, America as a whole needed a more honest dialogue about race—and that opposition to Black Lives Matter could squash that conversation. "When a person struggling with what's been broadcast on our airwaves says, 'black lives matter,' we should not say 'all lives matter' to justify ignoring the real need for change," Stephenson said.

At our 2017 annual conference, Stephenson admitted he wasn't sure he should touch this third rail of American life. After all, just 43 percent of Americans—and a mere 40 percent of white Americans—supported the Black Lives Matter movement as of mid-2016.[51] But Stephenson felt it was the right thing to do. And he was surprised by how much positive support he received—from people of all races. Stephenson got so many comments that it took him months to finish reading through them. "It just gave people permission to do something I think they were yearning and dying to do," Stephenson said. "It just picked at a raw nerve and said 'go have a conversation about this.'"

By taking a risk to abide by AT&T's principles and his own moral code, Stephenson not only helped employees—and the nation—have a more honest conversation about race. He also showed AT&T to be the kind of company that the public can be proud to do business with.

Many companies in recent decades have articulated value statements. And not all walk the talk. But rest assured, the public—employees, customers, and investors—eventually figures out what leaders and organizations actually believe. This can be seen in an intriguing study on our pool of Best Workplaces.

The 2013 study by scholars at the University of Chicago and two other research organizations found "proclaimed values" by companies appear irrelevant to their business results. But, the study found, a firm's performance is stronger when employees perceive top managers as trustworthy and ethical—two concepts typically included in values statements. In particular, the research into nearly 700 companies that completed our Trust Index Employee Survey found high levels of perceived management integrity are positively correlated with "higher productivity, profitability, better industrial relations, and higher level of attractiveness to prospective job applicants."[52]

In essence, when companies live out strong values, employees buy in figuratively while customers buy in literally. Given shifts in the business landscape toward a more purpose-conscious public, heightened transparency into companies, and increased expectations that business leaders will lead on social issues, meaningful values are only growing more valuable.

A Foundation of Trust

The final key to maximizing human potential and creating a company built for success is a foundation of trust. Trust is what we discovered to be the cornerstone of great workplaces 30 years ago. And trust—specifically, a relationship of trust between employees and leadership—remains as important today as it was then. That's because while business conditions have changed dramatically, people are still people. Trust is a universal requirement for positive interactions.

We also have discovered camaraderie among coworkers and a feeling of pride in the job are part of what makes for a great work experience. But trust, you might say, is first among equals. Without trust in leaders, camaraderie becomes an unhealthy us-versus-them bond, and pride in one's work develops in spite of misgivings about the organization, as a kind of consolation prize in an otherwise unpleasant situation. Camaraderie and pride find their best, fullest expression when trust is present too.

How do you build a high-trust culture? We believe the key elements of trust are credibility, respect, and fairness. Employees trust leaders when they see them as credible, as respectful, and as fair. As we discussed earlier in the chapter, leaders must behave in a scrupulously fair way and demonstrate respect to everyone in the organization. They also must show themselves to be competent in running the business and consistent in living up to their word.

Over time, we have seen that one of the first steps leaders should take to improve trust is to listen to employees—to ask how they are doing, and to involve them in decisions that affect them. But we have seen that beliefs matter too. If an executive doesn't believe that employees have worthy things to say, if they fundamentally believe they are better than those "under" them, if they think workers are at root lazy and duplicitous, it will be hard for them to cultivate trust. They may go through the motions of asking for employee viewpoints or recognizing their achievements but the leader's actions will come across as half-hearted and people will likely sniff out the insincerity.

In recent years, we have explored the optimal set of beliefs around trust. We have identified what we call the For All Trust Mindset, where people extend trust deeply and broadly. Leaders with this mindset aren't naïve. They don't give endless chances to low performers. But they tend to have faith in people and view mistakes with curiosity as opposed to condemnation. They give people the benefit of the doubt, regardless of who they are or what they do in the organization.

With the help of a For All Trust Mindset, leaders can build trust. They create a culture where trust doesn't just run vertically between employees and leaders. It also begins to flow horizontally among peers, which speeds up decisions and improves collaboration. Ultimately, trust fuels business performance. Decades of data prove the point. High-trust organizations enjoy high levels of employee engagement, stronger employee retention, stock market outperformance, and greater profitability, to name a few business benefits that we shared in Chapter 1.

In talking about Great Places to Work For All, the "For All" addition is about extending a great, high-trust climate and its benefits to everyone. By doing so, by closing the workplace gaps, organizations see an even greater business advantage. Trust fuels performance. For All accelerates it.

Innovation

When organizations maximize human potential through effective leadership, meaningful values, and a foundation of trust, good things happen. One of them is innovation.

At a time when new competitors can spring up suddenly across the globe, organizations today must innovate. Innovate constantly—in terms of new products, new business lines, and new internal systems to optimize efficiency and profitability. And innovation is not just for technology companies. Industries as varied as hospitality, retail, and financial services are facing disruptions. Financial services firms, for example, face competition from passively managed funds and "roboadvisors" attractive to many millennials, while the rise of cryptocurrencies and other alternative payment technologies are posing a threat to the biggest players.[53]

So innovation is vital. But your grandfather's approach to innovation won't cut it. The prevailing wisdom over the past few decades has been an exclusive approach to invention: set up a research and development team or other "skunk works" group charged with formulating the next big thing. There's nothing wrong in putting brilliant minds to work on innovation activities. But in recent years, it has become clear that listening to the "wisdom of the crowd" and seeking good ideas from everywhere leads to better results.

What's needed today is what might be called Innovation By All. That is, tapping the insights and ideas of employees from every level of the organization. At Quicken Loans, for example, members of the technology team can take four hours of "bullet time" weekly to work on personal projects outside their normal responsibilities. Quicken also offers prizes at a company-wide pitch day to solicit ideas from employees—a practice more associated with tech than finance and one that fosters innovation to address current issues facing the firm.[54]

Famed design shop Ideo has similar findings on how to cultivate successful innovation. According to Ideo, keys to an innovative, adaptive company include "empowerment" that affects "all corners of the company" and collaboration across business functions "to approach opportunities and challenges from all angles."[55] These conclusions dovetail with other research on the power of diverse perspectives to generate better breakthroughs.[56]

Our latest research also points to the power of a For All culture on innovation and business results. Using our Trust Index Employee Survey, we created an index of what we call the Innovation Experience. It measures the extent to which all employees participate in activities related to innovation, experience leadership behaviors that foster experimentation, and feel inspired to move the organization forward. The results are striking. When we examined several hundred Great Place to Work–Certified companies, those in the top quartile on the Innovation Experience index had revenue growth more than three times the revenue growth of those in the bottom quartile (see Figure 11). In other words, the organizations that best promote an Innovation By All culture leap ahead of the competition.

It's also important to note what happens today if you don't cultivate an Innovation By All climate. Those great ideas walk out the door. Sometimes the people with the ideas create their own start-up—possibly a new competitor. The agility of the modern worker to move from place to place means they don't have to wait for their organization to realize the time is ripe for their idea—they can go make it happen when they're ready.

So how do you execute a more decentralized innovation strategy? For one thing, it requires employees who feel encouraged and inspired to bring their ideas forward. This is best done in a climate of trust. Emma Seppala, a Stanford psychologist, has found a culture of trust, rather than fear,

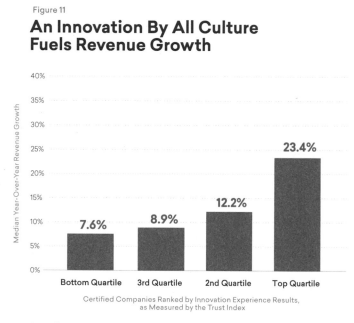

Figure 11

An Innovation By All Culture Fuels Revenue Growth

Certified Companies Ranked by Innovation Experience Results,
as Measured by the Trust Index

Source: Great Place to Work analysis

encourages collaboration and builds a creative workplace. If employees are afraid of being punished, they are far less likely to take chances, which is essential to innovation.[57]

But companies today need to go a step farther than building trust *overall* if they want optimum innovation. For Innovation By All, organizations need to maximize all their human potential. They need to create a culture that is great For All—an inclusive, high-trust culture where everyone is having a great experience and buys into advancing the organization.

Examples from the sports world drive this point home. During the 2015 NBA finals series, the Golden State Warriors were searching for ways to counter the Cleveland Cavaliers' star forward LeBron James. As discussed in Chapter 1, a pivotal idea came from one of the lowest-ranking members of coach Steve Kerr's staff. Coaching assistant Nick U'Ren proposed starting defensive specialist Andre Iguodala in place of center Andrew Bogut.[58] The idea was unconventional—it left the Warriors without the traditional center big man. But Kerr tried it, and it paid off. Iguodala helped shut down James, winning the Most Valuable Player award of the finals series as Golden State won the championship.

During the 2017 professional football championship, the New England Patriots pulled off the biggest-ever comeback in Super Bowl history in part by listening to the players on the field. "We made some adjustments," Patriot's defensive coordinator Matt Patricia said after the game. "[Our defensive backs] do a good job of coming back and giving us feedback. I think those guys understand the game to a level that I don't think anybody really comprehends. They'll come back and say, 'Hey, we see this, we think we can do this, maybe let's make this adjustment,' and that's what they did."[59]

The kind of bottom-up innovation you increasingly see in the sports world is the same that's needed in business today. And it's what you get at a Great Place to Work For All.

Financial Growth

You also get to grow your business faster. A lot faster.

This may seem like crazy talk, given that most leaders do everything they can to increase revenue. But there's a secret weapon that many business executives fail to use: people power. People power means truly tapping the full potential of all your workers, regardless of who they are and what they do for the organization. As we discussed in Chapter 1, when organizations create a consistently great work experience, they see revenue accelerate by a factor of more than three. That extra growth comes from people who are bringing their best to their jobs, thinking up new and better services in their spare time, and going out of their way—with a smile on their face—to serve your customers well.

In other words, through the power of your people you can make the revenue pie bigger.

This is crucial today because businesses need a surplus of cash. We live in an economy that is turbulent and, in the words of McKinsey researchers, "growing more unpredictable."[60] In such a business climate, organizations without the growth to generate a prudent cash reserve are at significant risk. Companies need a buffer to invest in new products and services and to prepare for rainy days when revenues may take a sudden hit.

Businesses should be mindful of hypergrowth. There's a calculation regarding an organization's optimal "sustainable growth rate," which refers to how quickly it can grow without borrowing more money.[61] Organizations can get into trouble when they expand in such a way that expectations push employees past their breaking point and become unhealthy. Or when rapid growth excuses poor behavior. Look no further than Uber and how its "Always be hustlin'" value, combined with a macho culture and focus on growth, contributed to a toxic workplace internally and ultimately a backlash from customers and investors.

Still, an expanding revenue pie and healthy cash reserves are vital to all companies, and especially so for Great Places to Work For All. Growth is needed to pay to help people develop, to compensate them fairly, to show them respect and appreciation in the form of things like all-company celebrations. There's a virtuous cycle at play: revenue growth helps create a great work experience for everyone. And by investing in people power, companies see strong business results.

A New Era, a New Definition of Greatness

This portrait of a great workplace marks a change for us. We haven't lost our focus on the employee experience, but we realized we needed to widen our lens.

In the economy that's taking shape, one in which more people expect to be included and expect more of companies, in which business agility is at a premium, and in which "hired hearts" are vital to success, we needed to update our definition of a great place to work.

We realized we needed to raise the bar. What was good enough to be great is no longer good enough. The gaps at the Best Workplaces aren't great for the people experiencing a less-than-great culture. And they aren't great for the organizations either. So we needed to add maximizing human potential to the foundation of trust. We also needed to call out values and leadership effectiveness as other key components. And note that innovation and financial growth are what you get when all these pieces are in place. Taken together, this is what we see when we talk about Great Places to Work For All; Organizations that are better for business, better for people, and better for the world.

While all six elements are vital to a Great Place to Work

For All, maximizing human potential is at the heart of our new definition. It can make or break a company's greatness in the emerging economy. Our data shows as much.

In the next chapter, we'll explore just how much better business results can be when an organization truly is great for everyone: how maximizing human potential accelerates performance.

Chapter 4
Maximizing Human Potential Accelerates Performance

Closing gaps in employees' workplace experience accelerates business performance in terms of higher revenue, better stock performance, and improved retention.

As outlined in the previous chapters, in the emerging economy companies are under pressure to bring out the best in all their employees in order to survive and thrive. Everyone counts in a business climate defined by heightened expectations on the part of employees and customers, radical transparency, rapid change, and decentralized decision making.

To realize the full potential of all employees requires that all employees have a great experience at work—no matter who they are or what they do for the organization. This way, all people show up to work inspired, ready to collaborate, ready to adapt and learn, willing to put themselves on the line for the organization and its mission to advance.

In short, organizations face a business imperative to create a consistently great place to work. Unfortunately, most companies today fall short of this goal. Even at the best workplaces, there are gaps in the workplace experience.[62] By "gaps," we mean that some workers have a less positive experience at work than others, based on who they are or what they do for the company.

Close the Gaps, Accelerate Performance

In this chapter, we'll take a look at the workplace gaps facing particular demographic groups—executives and non-executives; women and men; baby boomers and millennials; whites and minorities—and the economic impact of failing to foster the full potential of the people in those categories. Some of the places where companies are falling short as a result of these gaps are in stock market performance, employee retention, productivity, and brand ambassadorship. In other words, where gaps exist, money is being left on the table.

Traditionally, the idea of widening the lens to include all employees' human potential hasn't been taken very seriously by business leaders. Instead, a big focus has been placed on identifying and grooming "high-potential" employees only. To be sure, different employees contribute different amounts of value to a company's success. But in the kind of economy that is emerging, optimal performance requires every person in the organization to plug in with energy, ideas, and a solid understanding of the company's goals. Think of the Hyatt room service worker who became the highlight of a couple's trip by listening, engaging, and sharing his singing talents each night.

That employee took his game to the next level, bolstering Hyatt's business in the form of great customer service along the way. And he could do so only because Hyatt has done so much to close the gap between executives and rank-and-file workers. It has given them real authority to make judgment calls that drive outstanding customer service, it has invited them to bring their full selves to work, and it has created a culture of recognizing great performance.

That's what Great Places to Work For All do on a grand scale when they close the gaps—when they maximize human potential. When great workplaces reach everybody, everybody reaches higher. Going back to the Golden State Warriors, look at coaching assistant Nick U'Ren. The crucial suggestion by the then-28-year-old to start Andre Iguodala in the 2015 finals wasn't a mere whim. U'Ren first expressed the notion over a team dinner, but it got a lukewarm reception. So he did more research, studying films of the previous year's finals series involving LeBron James. He saw a similar strategy succeed, convinced assistant coach Luke Walton to back the switch to Iguodala, and then U'Ren and Walton sent a text with the idea to head coach Steve Kerr at 3 a.m.[63]

In other words, U'Ren went above and beyond the call of duty, and raised his own game. And that performance cannot be isolated from the Warriors' culture of respect, where, as Kerr put it, "We have a staff that is very cooperative. Whoever has the idea, it doesn't matter."

These sorts of anecdotes are backed by a growing mound of evidence showing that equitable environments that maximize human potential score big. A 2015 study by research firm Bersin by Deloitte found that companies that focus on leadership and inclusion in their talent strategies outperform peers on a variety of business measures, including:

> 2.3 times higher cash flow per employee over a three-year period
> 1.8 times more likely to be change-ready

> 1.7 times more likely to be innovation leaders in their market[64]

Our own research comes to similar conclusions. For example, we found Great Places to Work For All outperformed the S&P 500 in the stock market—considerably.

We studied the stock performance of publicly traded companies that participated in the 2017 FORTUNE 100 Best competition, applying the new Great Place to Work For All Score methodology. As mentioned in Chapter 1, the For All Score moves beyond the average level of trust in the company. It is a composite measure of how positively and consistently employees rate their workplace on metrics related to innovation, leadership effectiveness, and trust, regardless of who they are and what they do within their organization.

We then created a mock stock portfolio of the publicly traded companies that ranked in the top 100 For All organizations according to the new methodology (referred to here as the For All 100) and assessed their performance against the S&P 500 Index. Over the past three and five years, the publicly traded For All 100 significantly outpaced the S&P 500 (see Figure 12).

The average annual return for the publicly traded For All 100 over the past three years was 51.4 percent—nearly 50 percent better than the S&P 500 performance over the same period.

The publicly traded For All 100 did even better against the S&P 500 over the past five years. With a mean annual return of 146.4 percent, the publicly traded For All 100 performed 62 percent better than the S&P 500.

Figure 12

Great Places to Work For All Beat the S&P 500

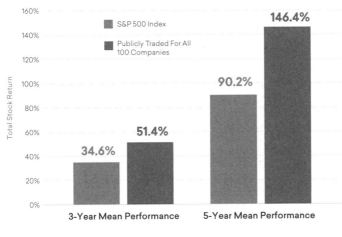

S&P 500 Index

Publicly Traded For All 100 Companies

Total Stock Return

160%
140%
120%
100%
80%
60%
40%
20%
0%

34.6%

51.4%

90.2%

146.4%

3-Year Mean Performance   5-Year Mean Performance

Source: Great Place to Work analysis

As we mentioned in Chapter 1, For All companies also race ahead on revenue. Businesses in the top quartile on For All metrics enjoy more than three times the revenue growth of companies in the bottom quartile. And we have seen that Great Places to Work For All grow faster than companies that simply show high levels of trust on average.

Our latest research reaffirms that a high level of trust overall fuels growth, but it also shows a For All workplace accelerates that growth.

Different Groups of Employees Have Different Gaps to Close

These broader findings illustrate that it's clearly in an organization's best interest that everyone in the organization is having an optimal experience. Where there are gaps, there are places where human potential is leaking out of the company, diminishing the strength of the organization.

We set out to find where gaps exist between different groups of employees, so that leaders know where to start focusing their energy to close these gaps. We did this by looking at the survey results from a pool of Great Place to Work–Certified companies, in which more than 225,000 employees were surveyed.

We should note that these companies are among the best workplaces in the United States. At Great Place to Work–Certified workplaces, at least 7 of 10 employees at the company say their company is a great place to work. All of these companies have relatively high levels of trust, pride, and camaraderie overall. But a deeper look at the data shows that even at these organizations the work experience isn't always consistent—and that gaps in experience often aligned to an employee's personal characteristics or job role.

Most striking were the significant gaps that emerged in specific areas across the four major categories noted earlier: gender, generational cohorts, racial/ethnic groups, and job level. Interestingly, the gaps varied in nature based on demographic category. For example, on average, even among these great workplaces, women do not have a say at work to the extent men do. Minority employees don't experience the same level of community at work as their white counterparts. Older workers are not having as much fun at work or being included in decisions to the extent younger workers are. Frontline employees are not as valued, nor do they feel that their work has meaning as often as leaders do.

If we extrapolate these results across the broader U.S. and world, those gaps amount to wasted human potential for millions of people, and to unrealized revenue in thousands of organizations. In fact, of all the elements of a Great Place to Work For All, the human potential piece is the most pivotal— the area where companies can most improve their performance. This isn't mere rhetoric or speculation. We have begun to collect data that quantifies these workplace experience gaps and just how much companies stand to gain by closing them. Here is what we are learning.

Leaders Versus Individual Contributors: It's Good to Be Queen

Of all the workplace gaps we found, the largest are between employees across different job levels. Put simply, the higher you go in the organization, the better the work experience tends to be.

This makes sense on an intuitive level. After all, executives call the shots and make the most money. But the natural outcomes of being an executive, which include greater influence and decision-making power as well as a heftier paycheck, have broader implications on *all* employees' experience at a great workplace: things like feeling they make a difference at work, feeling valued, and believing the workplace is fair. Executives' ability to effectively manage the realities of their position of power becomes critical to closing the gaps and creating a great workplace for all employees.

These findings also illustrate the blind spot many executives have about what's really going on in their companies. Our survey is not just about employees' own experiences—it also assesses what they think happens in the company at large. For example, 81 percent of executives (versus 64 percent of individual contributors) reported they believe they *personally* receive their fair share of the company's profit. These numbers are simply a collective report of each employee's *own* experience. However, when we asked respondents whether "people here are paid fairly for the work they do," this goes beyond the individual employee's own experience and asks them to reflect on the company's practices at large, for everyone. For this statement, we uncovered a blind spot for executives. While 85 percent of executives believed people at their company were paid fairly for their work, this number dropped 15 points to 70 percent among individual contributors.

This data suggests executives need to listen more closely to people at all levels of the company because they are not always aware of potential issues in the organization—including experiences that influence productivity, engagement, and innovation.

Key Gaps Between Job Levels: Fairness, Communication, and Meaningful Work

Between each of the job levels—executives (including executive and C-level leaders), managers (including middle managers, frontline managers, and supervisors), and individual contributors—our data revealed that fairness was the most prominent gap. This includes perceptions of fair pay and profit sharing, fairness in promotions, perceptions of favoritism, access to a fair appeals process, and more.

Another consistent gap that emerged is around employees feeling they are included in decisions that affect them. Individual contributors and managers alike are far less likely than executives to believe that they are involved in decisions that affect their job or work environment, or that managers genuinely seek and respond to their suggestions and ideas.

We also found a telling gap between executives and mid-level managers specifically. Mid-level managers are far less likely than executives to believe that leaders make expectations clear, keep people informed about important issues and changes, or do a good job assigning and coordinating resources.

Taken together, these gaps in communication and decision making are bad news for an organization. When middle managers, who serve as the critical linchpin between executives and individual contributors, are not well informed, they cannot effectively connect employees to the broader rationale that drives decisions, or to the company's overall goals and strategy. When employees across the board feel that leaders do not actively seek their input or ideas, especially on decisions that affect them directly, they are more likely to feel that decisions are happening "to" them, rather than something they had the opportunity to be a part of. Employees may also have valuable frontline information that would help leaders understand how a change would affect the company's operations or customers. Instead, employees are often left in the dark, unable to effectively support the company's goals.

To be sure, leaders can't include all employees in every decision or keep them updated on every change at every moment. However, these gaps are important to mitigate. It's far more difficult to speed forward if employees put up blocks to decisions that catch them off guard or if they don't have enough information to do their jobs. Also, when leaders take the time to build trust by including employees, those workers are more likely to give leaders the benefit of the doubt when they do lack information, and assume good intentions.

For individual contributors, specifically, some other key gaps emerged as well. Among them were lower results for feeling their work has special meaning, feeling that management shows a sincere interest in them as people, not just employees, and having equal access to opportunities for recognition. If we combine these gaps with the ones noted above regarding unfair perceptions of pay, profit sharing, and promotions, as well as being excluded from decision making and idea sharing, this amounts to a far less rewarding experience for employees who are not in management or leadership roles—one that may leave them feeling like a replaceable "cog in the wheel" rather than a valued member of the team.

Again, these gaps have damaging implications for the business. For example, our research shows among millennial individual contributors specifically, those who report that their managers show a sincere interest in them as people are eight times more likely to demonstrate qualities related to change readiness, agility, and innovation.

The Value of Closing Job-Level Gaps

Some might argue that these gaps are inevitable, the natural order of things. And perhaps it is impossible to completely eliminate workplace differences between the top decision makers of an organization and others working there. But our data shows that some companies are much better at creating a consistent experience whether one works in a 70th floor C-suite penthouse, a 20th floor cubicle, or a basement boiler room. And those companies are outperforming their peers.

Figure 13

Close the Gap between Leaders and Employees, See Revenue Soar

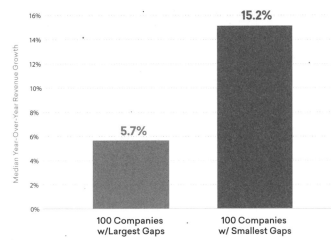

Source: Great Place to Work analysis

Figure 13 shows the revenue growth among companies with large versus small gaps between leaders (which includes executives and managers at all levels) and individual contributors. These results are drawn from a study of several hundred Great Place to Work–Certified companies of different sizes, industries, and geographies.

The first data set represents the 100 companies from the group with the largest gaps on our Trust Index Survey between leaders' scores and individual contributors' scores. The second set is the 100 companies with the smallest gaps.

As Figure 13 shows, companies with the narrowest gap between leaders and non-leaders had an annual revenue growth

Figure 14

Retention, Brand Ambassadorship, and Productivity Increase as Leader–Employee Gap Shrinks

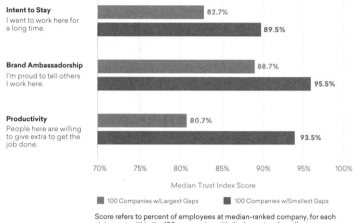

Intent to Stay
I want to work here for a long time.
82.7%
89.5%

Brand Ambassadorship
I'm proud to tell others I work here.
88.7%
95.5%

Productivity
People here are willing to give extra to get the job done.
80.7%
93.5%

70%   75%   80%   85%   90%   95%   100%

Median Trust Index Score

■ 100 Companies w/Largest Gaps   ■ 100 Companies w/Smallest Gaps

Score refers to percent of employees at median-ranked company, for each statement, within the 100 companies with the largest and smallest gaps.

Source: Great Place to Work analysis

rate nearly three times that of the companies with the widest chasm in experience between the two groups.

Accelerated revenue growth isn't the only benefit of a more equal experience among employees of different job levels. We also found higher productivity, brand ambassadorship, and intent to stay at the companies that best close the gap between the top and bottom of the organization. For example, as seen in Figure 14, at the 100 companies with the smallest gaps between leaders and individual contributors, nearly 94 percent of the workforce reports that people are willing to give extra to get the job done. That compares to 81 percent at the companies with the biggest divides between the top and bottom layers of the company. And nearly 96 percent of employees at companies with the smallest management–individual contributor gaps are proud to tell others they work at their organization, up from 89 percent at companies with the largest gaps.

While the numbers may appear strong overall, it is still a gap, and those 7 percentage points in brand ambassadorship amount to an unnecessary organizational leak—one that only becomes exacerbated in an era of employees living out their lives on social media. Performance suffers when a less-than-optimal portion of your employees speak proudly about your brand. Combine that missed opportunity with higher-than-necessary turnover and fewer staff members giving their all, and the impact of this leak becomes evident. The organizations with the narrower gaps between leaders and rank-and-file employees are zipping ahead. These findings dovetail with other research on workplace experience and business results. Among the results our Trust Index captures is "employee engagement"—typically defined as an employee's desire to stay at their organization and their willingness to give extra on the job. Other studies have found engagement levels increase as an employee's job level increases, that engagement for most employees is low, and that increased engagement improves a variety of business outcomes.[65] Our conclusions about increased equality boosting business results are echoed in growing amounts of research at the societal level. As we'll discuss more in Chapter 6, evidence suggests that inequality hurts economic growth for countries overall.[66] The takeaway is clear: treating a great work experience as a perk or privilege of more senior roles is risky business. Create a more equitable experience at work among leaders and individual contributors and see your performance take off.

Men and Women: It's Good to Be Queen—and Better to Be King

If you have a daughter, pay special attention to this section. Because the truth is, while it's good to be queen, our data shows it's still far better to be king. And unless leaders around the world make it a priority for women to have a more equitable experience at work, there isn't much hope for the girls of today when they enter the workplace of tomorrow.

Pay inequities between genders have dominated the headlines for the past few years, and for good reason: it's common knowledge that women make 80 cents for every dollar made by men.[67] However, our research uncovered that the gender pay gap is just the tip of the iceberg.

Key Gaps in Access to Leadership, Being Treated as Valuable Contributors, and Fairness

On average, women and men in fairly equal numbers report an overall positive experience of the workplace across the companies we looked at. However, when we dug more deeply into the results, we found significant gaps in key areas. For starters, men are more likely than women to report more open lines of communication to managers and leaders. This includes being able to ask managers a reasonable question and getting a straight answer, being involved in decisions, and an overall sense that leaders are approachable.

Our findings dovetail with recent research on issues of gender, authority, and communication in organizations. Facebook executive Sheryl Sandberg and author Adam Grant synthesized some of this scholarship in a series of *New York Times* essays. Sandberg and Grant noted that women in organizations not only can find themselves interrupted when they speak up, but often are judged as overly aggressive for making their voice heard. "Women who worry that talking 'too much' will cause them to be disliked are not paranoid," Sandberg and Grant wrote. "They are often right."[68]

Men were also far more likely than women to be acknowledged and rewarded for their work—and not just when it comes to a fair paycheck. We found big gaps between men and women on their perceptions of fair pay, fair promotions, and equal opportunities for recognition.

Finally, women were more likely to experience a biased and unfair workplace in general. Not only are they more likely to perceive favoritism and unfair treatment based on gender, but they also report less access to a fair appeals process. Employees from several Great Place to Work–Certified companies have shared comments with us that capture the way sexism can exist even in an otherwise great workplace:

> "Many senior-level roles are occupied by men who appear to come from similar backgrounds, and their 'deputies' historically have been women. Men also in meetings are often the ones who are given the floor to explain a 'vision' or overall strategy rather than an operational or tactical element."

> "I feel that women are treated differently in leadership. Even interns that visit have noticed this. Men talk over women, they seem to be able to say and do whatever they want without repercussion…essentially the good old boys club. It's tough to be a female leader around here."

> "Looking at our Sr. Leadership, there are women. However, the string of degrees behind their name suggests that they have had to work twice as hard to prove themselves. Very few of the men possess this level of education."

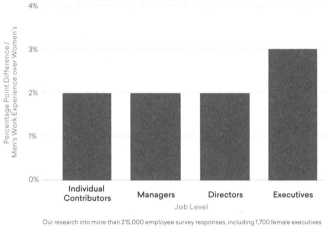

Figure 15

The Gender Gap Widens at the Top

Our research into more than 215,000 employee survey responses, including 1,700 female executives and 3,200 male executives, found the widest workplace experience gap between men and women happens at the executive level.

Source: Great Place to Work analysis

These employee comments speak to a striking finding we recently made about women and men as they progress up the corporate ladder: the workplace gender gap is greatest at the top. There is a difference in overall experience between male and female employees at every level of the organization, and both men and women have an increasingly positive experience at higher levels of management. But the gap between the sexes is largest among executives and the C-suite, according to our research in preparing the 2017 Best Workplaces for Women ranking (see Figure 15).

Something appears to change in that most rarified air in organizations, such that female executives have a significantly different experience than their male peers in corner offices.

This particular finding dovetails with a recent *New York Times* article by Susan Chira about challenges women face in reaching the very pinnacle of organizations. The lack of CEO women isn't about "the pipeline" of talent but about "loneliness, competition and deeply rooted barriers," according to the story.[69]

These experiences find support in our Best Workplaces for Women research. We discovered that the gap in perceptions of favoritism between men and women was largest at the executive level. So was the gap on perceptions of a psychologically healthy climate. While 80 percent of female executives called their workplace psychologically and emotionally healthy, 87 percent of men did.

The upshot of this gap is that organizations are squandering potential in their executive ranks. That's in part by diminishing the experience of women executives, but also by deterring more women from getting to the CEO role itself. Research indicates that women-led organizations outperform peers.[70] But many companies, through less than fully fair or welcoming climates for women in the C-suite, are blocking the benefits of female leadership.

Work–Life Balance: Not a "Women's Issue"

Another interesting finding in our research was a gap that did *not* emerge between men and women: work–life balance. While work–life balance was important to women, it was just as important to men. This wasn't surprising to us, because we found the same thing in researching and ranking the 2016 100 Best Workplaces for Women.

But corporate America and the general public still define

workplace flexibility and balance as something for female employees—especially for working mothers. By making work–life balance a women's issue, the damage is twofold: it crowds out other matters where real disparities exist between genders, and it neglects the fact that work–life balance is a real concern for men as well.

The Value of Closing Gender Gaps

As we saw with job levels, there is also value in closing the gender gaps. Overall, when the gaps between the genders shrink, we see an uptick in productivity, brand ambassadorship, and retention, which makes sense. If women make up half of a company's workforce, of course a company will perform better when half of employees have better access to information, are able to contribute their best ideas, and feel equally valued for their contributions.

On the issue of retention specifically, we have found women are three times more likely to want to stay with the company if management involves them in decisions that affect their jobs, and if they can ask management questions and get straight answers. They are also four times more likely to want to stay if they believe management is approachable and easy to talk with.

On the issue of fair pay, we can look to Salesforce for a case study on how closing gender gaps pays off. As mentioned in Chapter 1, Salesforce CEO Marc Benioff and his team invested $3 million in 2015 to address a gender pay gap. This action, in conjunction with other efforts to make all employees feel fully valued and included, has had striking results.

» In 2014, 84 percent of women at Salesforce felt pay was
  fair at the company, compared to 91 percent of men.
  By 2016, the share of women experiencing fair pay had
  climbed to 90 percent.

» The focus on leveling up women didn't make men feel
  overlooked—91 percent of men at the company continued
  to believe people get paid fairly.

» For both genders, levels of pride and brand ambassadorship climbed slightly such that 97 percent of both men
  and women now feel proud to tell others they work at
  Salesforce.

» The percentage of women employees who say they want
  to work at Salesforce for a long time has jumped from 85
  percent in 2014 to 93 percent.

Salesforce continues to work on the issue. In 2017, the
company conducted another, wider assessment on pay equality, evaluating salaries and bonuses globally. It also looked at
differences in pay for not only gender but also race and ethnic-
ity in the United States. Eleven percent of employees received
adjustments following the company's second assessment, and
Salesforce spent approximately $3 million more to address
any unexplained differences in pay.

"The need for another adjustment underscores the nature of pay equity—it is a moving target, especially for growing companies in competitive industries," Cindy Robbins,
Salesforce's executive vice president for employee success,
wrote in a blog about the 2017 effort. "It must be consistently monitored and addressed. Salesforce will continue to
focus on equality, diversity and inclusion at all levels, and

we plan to review employee compensation on an ongoing basis."[71]

This commitment to paying people fairly has gone hand in hand with strong business results at Salesforce. The company has been growing faster than its rivals and at the time of this writing dominated the customer relationship management arena with nearly twice the market share of its nearest competitor.[72]

Racial/Ethnic Minorities Compared with White Employees

The area of diversity and inclusion (D&I) has emerged as one of the hottest topics in the business world in the past few years. The D&I field refers, in large part, to fair treatment of racial and ethnic minorities in organizations. Heightened attention to racial equality in the work world may have something to do with the growing body of research on the business advantages of diversity. It may also stem from our polarized national climate, where racial extremists have grown bolder and sparked a reaction from leaders in many social sectors, including business.

In any event, much of the attention to organizational diversity has remained focused on the representation of different ethnicities. Our research suggests the conversation must go deeper. We have found that it is not enough to look at statistics on how many black, Latino, Asian American, and other people of color a company may have. It's vital also to explore the kind of experience those employees are having, relative to white employees. The experiential data will uncover the root causes of workplace gaps and enable practical decisions for creating a more consistent experience. Doing so contributes to an equitable society and is smart business strategy: when organizations close the gaps between racial groups, performance improves.

Key Gaps in Fairness, Responsibility Level, and Being a Part of a Caring Community

On the whole, the employees in our study who identified as a racial or ethnic minority have a less positive experience than their white counterparts in key areas of fairness such as promotions, fair pay, and fair treatment regardless of race, whereas whites were far less likely than minorities to perceive racism at work. We also discovered additional areas where minorities did not enjoy as positive a workplace as whites. In particular, one of the largest gaps between the racial groups had to do with whether employees felt that people in the organization care about each other, with minorities being significantly less likely than whites to feel they're part of a caring community. This disparity was echoed by two other key differences: people feeling welcome when they switch job units, and management hiring people who fit in well. The picture that emerges is one where fewer minorities feel a strong sense of community at work as compared to their white colleagues.

What's interesting about this finding is that the Great Place to Work–Certified companies in the study are defined, in part, by their caring communities. It may come as a surprise to leaders of these firms to learn that some colleagues are not having that same experience, based on their race. The caring community that the dominant white group believes everyone feels part of actually doesn't feel that way for everyone.

Another striking gap is that minorities are less likely than whites to believe they are given a lot of responsibility (84 percent of minorities versus 90 percent of whites).

Collectively, these gaps along racial lines suggest that, as with women, minority groups can feel like second-class citizens in the workplace. They experience less fair treatment, are given fewer opportunities to demonstrate their value, and are not as welcomed into a caring community of colleagues. And while these are the primary gaps that we found, it should be noted that whites had a more positive experience than minority employees across 56 of the 58 statements on our Trust Index Survey—with the remaining two statements at a veritable tie between the groups. It's apparent, in other words, that even at the Best Workplaces, people of color have a consistently less positive experience across the board.

The Value of Closing Racial Gaps

So other than the obvious moral reasons for doing so, why should a company try to close these racial gaps?

For one thing, a portion of your workforce feeling less care than others crimps growth. Some readers may doubt that the "soft" issue of caring at work could have hard-edged business implications. But we have found that employees experiencing a caring community at work is one of the top drivers of revenue outperformance for small and medium companies. In particular, when employees in a high-trust culture experience a caring workplace, they are *44 percent more likely* to work for a company with above-average revenue growth.[73]

Likewise, the racial gaps in fairness and levels of responsibility are red flags for business results. Employees are less

Figure 16
Close Racial Gaps, Grow Revenue

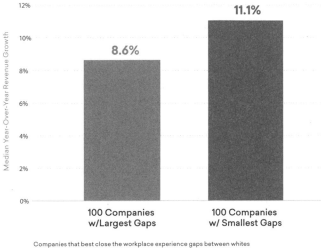

Companies that best close the workplace experience gaps between whites and racial minorities have roughly 30% higher revenue growth.

Source: Great Place to Work analysis

likely to be fully engaged or productive if they perceive an unequal playing field, one where they are less welcome to play an important role.

The numbers bear out this analysis. In our examination of Great Place to Work–Certified companies, we found the 100 companies with the largest gaps between the experiences of white employees and minorities had significantly lower revenue growth than the 100 companies with the smallest gaps. As Figure 16 shows, the companies with the largest gaps had 8.6 percent revenue growth, while the top quartile had 11.1 percent growth. In other words, the companies with the most consistently positive experience between minority and white

Figure 17

Retention, Brand Ambassadorship, and Productivity Increase as Racial Gaps Shrink

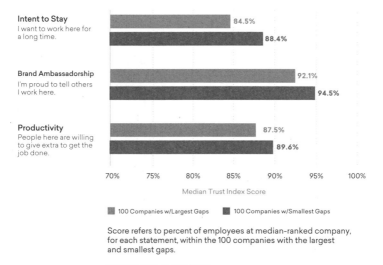

Intent to Stay
I want to work here for a long time.
84.5%
88.4%

Brand Ambassadorship
I'm proud to tell others I work here.
92.1%
94.5%

Productivity
People here are willing to give extra to get the job done.
87.5%
89.6%

70%   75%   80%   85%   90%   95%   100%

Median Trust Index Score

■ 100 Companies w/Largest Gaps   ■ 100 Companies w/Smallest Gaps

Score refers to percent of employees at median-ranked company, for each statement, within the 100 companies with the largest and smallest gaps.

Source: Great Place to Work analysis

employees posted revenue growth nearly one-third greater over the same period.

And it doesn't end there. We also found employees' productivity, brand ambassadorship, and intent to stay also rise when racial gaps narrow (see Figure 17).

As mentioned earlier in the book, many previous studies have shown that demographically diverse teams improve business performance.[74] But our research here on revenue, productivity, brand ambassadorship, and intent to stay goes a step further. It indicates that the *relative experience* of racial and ethnic minorities—not just their mere presence—affects results. It matters how good people of color have it at work, as compared to white employees. When a positive experience is shared equitably across racial lines, the company as a whole benefits.

This isn't the first time we've seen as much in our data. In 2016, we found the most inclusive workplaces enjoyed annual revenue gains 24 percent higher than peers.[75] And, as mentioned in Chapter 1, employees' experience of genuine workplace inclusion—as seen by high, consistent survey scores in areas such as fair treatment and a caring environment—was a better predictor of revenue growth than headcount diversity alone.

Organizations get the full benefits of a diverse workforce not just by creating a more diverse workforce, but by creating a great workplace experience for people of all colors.

The Generation Gap: Multiple Generations Can Make One Great Business

Much gets made of the differences between the generations at work. But a surprising finding from a study of the 100 Best contestants is that the three major generations—baby boomers (employees born between 1946 and 1964), Gen Xers (1965 to 1980), and millennials (1981 onward)—reported roughly the same overall experience of most of the key elements that make up a great workplace. Eighty-seven percent of employees from each group reported their company was a great place to work often or almost all of the time. This is a testament to the ability of great workplaces to create a measure of consistency across age groups—despite the fact that employees are coming to the table from inherently different places, given their broader life stage. It also speaks to the way a foundation of trust, along with camaraderie and pride, produces a great work experience no matter one's age.

That said, we did find several notable differences between the groups that are worth mentioning.

Key Generation Gaps: Purpose and Pride

The biggest gaps, not surprisingly, were between baby boomers and millennials. Yet one of the gaps that may come as a surprise—given the attention millennials receive for craving meaningful work—was that boomers are actually more likely to feel a sense of purpose and pride in their work than their younger counterparts. More specifically, boomers are more likely than millennials to report that their work has special meaning, that they make a difference at work, and that they feel good about the ways they contribute to the community.

This "purpose gap" may have something to do with heightened expectations of millennials around meaning on the job. While all people want and need a sense of purpose at work, millennials have been noted as being more willing than their boomer counterparts to prioritize purpose over things like job security or a pay raise.[76] It also may be the case that organizations aren't doing as good a job explaining their mission and values to younger workers, and how the work of those younger employees connects to the organization's higher goals.

Whatever the exact cause, other research we've conducted suggests the purpose deficit relates to millennials' greater retention risk. Purpose, we have discovered, is a key component of employee retention.[77]

We also found areas where millennials are more likely to have a better experience at work than boomers. Millennials sense to a greater degree that promotions are fair, politicking is off-limits, and people are treated fairly regardless of their age. They are also more likely to experience a fun, family atmosphere and to believe they are included in decisions.

These findings are notable. As companies strive to create hip cultures that cater to the younger cohort, it's important not to inadvertently shun or exclude older employees and the value they bring. As one employee from a recognized great workplace shares: "Respect your employees regardless of their age. Long-time working employees are a great asset and their experience should be well respected."

The largest difference between boomers and millennials, and one that represents potentially the largest financial risk for organizations, is their intent to stay at the organization for the long haul. While 89 percent of boomers say they plan to work at their company "for a long time," just 79 percent of millennials we surveyed said the same. And according to our Best Workplaces for Millennials list, twice as many millennial leaders as boomer leaders are flight risks. This isn't entirely surprising, given their life stage; after all, millennials are less likely to be tied to employer-provided health insurance or the financial obligations of home ownership, for example.

However, millennials who say that their company is a great place to work are *20 times* more likely to say they'd like to stay with the company for a long time, as compared to millennial employees who do not experience a great workplace.

In other words, if you want to improve retention among millennial employees, give them a great workplace.

Closing the Generation Gap

As mentioned above, we don't see a significant difference regarding the *overall* level of trust that the three major generations experience at Great Place to Work–Certified companies. But in a number of key areas, there are gaps, and they are a drag on company performance. The biggest leak may relate to turnover among millennials. Roughly one in five millennials changed jobs within the last year, more than three times the number of non-millennials. The cost of millennial turnover due to low engagement is estimated to be $30.5 billion annually.[78]

Our research has found key drivers of millennial retention are areas where younger employees have a worse experience than their baby boomer peers: purpose, meaning, and pride. In particular, millennials are 12 times more likely to want to stay at their employer for a long time if they feel they make a difference at work, feel their job has special meaning, and feel good about the ways the organization contributes to the community. When millennial employees are proud to tell others about their company, they are 19 times more likely to plan a long-term future with the organization. Close the purpose–pride generation gap, and see millennials propel your organization forward.

Creating a great workplace for millennials is a pressing matter when it comes to leadership levels in particular. As we mentioned in Chapter 2, millennials' overall experience declines as they move into senior leadership ranks. This represents a risk for the future of many companies. Young executives, who've received expensive training and developed significant institutional knowledge, could well leave for greener pastures if a promotion amounts to a decline in their quality of life. The good news, though, is that companies can keep millennials if they provide a great, high-trust culture. The key is to ensure millennials' experience stays positive as they rise to the highest leadership levels.

Going in the other generational direction, there's a key gap that bodes poorly for businesses. As noted above, baby boomers have lower perceptions that managers involve people in decisions that affect them, and that leaders genuinely seek and respond to suggestions. But these employees are more likely to bring a vast reservoir of life experience and career knowledge to the table that should not be ignored. Decentralized decision making and a climate that encourages idea sharing are vital to the kind of involve-everyone agility needed to thrive in business today. If older employees experience more of a command-and-control culture, they will not bring forth their best ideas. That reticence results in a leak—a leak companies will want to fix to maximize their growth and potential.

A Better Experience for All Is a Worthy Goal

Enabling everyone, no matter who they are or what they do, to have as great an experience as those most benefitting from work today is a worthy, moral, humanistic goal—one we'll talk more about in Chapters 5 and 6. But as we've seen, there's also hard business logic for shrinking the differences among groups in the workplace.

It's also important to note that other demographic groups besides the ones addressed here should not be neglected. Groups like remote workers, LGBTQ employees, former veterans, even introverts. It's vital not to lose sight of the fact that everyone is their own unique individual, despite being a part of a broader demographic group.

The bottom line is this: any person left behind in a company culture is bad for business. Each person, and their potential, matters. You will build the most hopeful future for your organization by including everyone.

Better for People, Better for the World

Chapter 5

When the Workplace Works for Everyone

At Great Places to Work For All, all employees are able to bring the best of themselves, even as they enjoy healthier, more fulfilling lives.

I look forward to coming to work every day. I do my best to recognize and do what needs to be done without being told. I do these things because Matrix has made an investment in me and my future. It is a friendly environment and is conducive to learning. They teach me core values that help me to live a better life and be a more positive person.

— EMPLOYEE, MATRIX SERVICE COMPANY

I love coming to work and interacting with my team and other employees. The policies are fair and we are always treated respectfully. We are given tasks that are meaningful, rewarding, and, for the most part, can make us feel like we are making a difference. I don't feel like I'm coming to a job; I feel like this part of my life is an extension of my family. It really makes it easy to come in and put everything into my work here.

— EMPLOYEE, SYNCHRONY FINANCIAL

This organization is more than a job to me, it's my life. My coworkers are my family. I identify as an O.C. Tanner employee and if I were to lose that I would lose a piece of myself.

— EMPLOYEE, O.C. TANNER

These are actual quotes from employees who work at recognized great places to work.[79] These people are having the quintessential experience of a great workplace, meaning they trust the people they work for, have pride in the work they do, and enjoy the people they work with. And this experience clearly has an impact on their broader lives in a powerful way. Notably, these people genuinely enjoy their jobs—contrary to the reported experience of most people on the planet. Each year since 2000, Gallup has famously reported that just under one-third of U.S. employees are engaged at work.[80] This number drops to a mere 15 percent on a global scale.[81]

Simply put, for most people, the way we work just isn't working, and as we have seen in the previous chapters, when employees do not experience a great place to work, it has a negative impact on the bottom line. But what is the impact on employees as people? Given we spend such a large amount of time at work (about one-third of our waking lives, assuming a 40-hour workweek), this poses a huge risk. Not just for the business, which leaves a lot on the table when employees are less than engaged, alive, and ready to contribute. It's also a problem for people. Over time, if the scale of bad days to good days at work tips in favor of the bad days, that can have a real impact on our overall quality of life—both in and out of the workplace.

Our experiences at work help shape who we are: our sense of self-worth, our overall enjoyment of life, our ability to reach our full potential. Our sense that we are making a difference with our time, that we can give the best of ourselves to something that matters. As Studs Terkel wrote in his seminal book *Working*, in which he interviewed people across professions

from taxicab driver to washroom attendant to business executive: "Work is about a search for daily meaning as well as daily
bread, for recognition as well as cash, for astonishment rather
than torpor; in short, for a sort of life rather than a Monday
through Friday sort of dying."[82]

Our research into the best workplaces over the past 30
years proves that work can indeed be a place where people
have a consistently positive, fulfilling experience that brings
out the best of who they are. At a Great Place to Work For All,
this is the primary experience of all people who work there—
regardless of who they are or what they do for the company.

A Human-Centric Workplace

In Chapter 2, we noted that business is in the midst of a shift
from a "knowledge economy" to a "human economy," where
success relies on human traits that can't be programmed into
software—traits such as creativity, passion, character, and
a collaborative spirit.[83] And though it may seem obvious, it's
worth noting that organizations can't benefit from the human
economy if they ask their employees to check what makes
them human at the door. People won't bring their passion,
creativity, and character to work if their true nature is stifled;
they can't offer a collaborative spirit if they're not part of a
community that welcomes and respects them.

Often, the idea of "perks and benefits" is confused with
a workplace that treats people well. Back to the quotes above,
note that there's no mention of perks. Bringing dry cleaning
services or a taco truck in on Wednesdays are nice ways to
show employees you care, but these sorts of surface-level
gestures don't define what it means to build a human-centric

workplace. Rather, workplaces are better for people when they meet deeper, more fundamental needs that help to elevate who we are as people and as professionals. Because we spend so much time at work, the workplace is the one place in our lives where these needs should be met with gusto.

Here, we'll look at some of the ways great workplaces for all help elevate the human spirit: by treating all employees with a deeply rooted sense of respect, enabling everyone in the organization to reach new heights of achievement, building a caring community for employees, where all are welcomed and supported in bringing their full selves to work, and inspiring a sense of meaning.

For a human economy to thrive, we need to embrace the fact that first and foremost, *all* employees are human beings—nothing more and nothing less.

Where Housekeepers Are Heroes

What do you believe about your employees? How do you *truly believe* they deserve to be treated—each and every one of them?

Before you answer this question, stop and take a close look in the mirror: at your life's experience, at the steps you took to get where you are today, at what you believe to be true about leadership and about work. If you are a leader who believes you trust employees, do your company's policies, practices, and behaviors communicate that? For example, are there multiple levels of approval for a manager who wants to buy a laptop, even though that laptop is in their budget? Is there anything holding you back from treating every employee with the same level of respect you want for yourself? Your honest beliefs about your employees, for better or for worse, shape your actions toward them. And as a leader, your actions shape their experience of the workplace.

A great place to work *for* all is built on trust-based relationships *with* all, and there's nothing more fundamental to trust than a real sense of respect between leaders and employees—no matter who they are or what they do for the company. We know this based on three decades of research on companies of all sizes, industries, and corners of the globe. When respect is at play, the workplace can work for everyone.

Merriam-Webster defines respect as "high or special regard."[84] Looking at the word's etymology, "to respect" historically has meant "to treat with deferential regard or esteem."[85] At Great Place to Work, we define the respect employees feel at work as one of the three dimensions of trust (the other two being credibility and fairness) and describe it as how employees believe leaders treat them—as people and as professionals.

Given these definitions, we can see how the idea of "respect" can present challenges in a work setting, where competition, boundaries, hierarchy, and status are all real factors to contend with. To cultivate an atmosphere of constant respect at work across employee groups is far easier said than done. A mutual sense of respect between employees and leaders takes a certain mindset on the part of leaders—a mindset that starts with the *genuine belief* that all employees deserve to be treated with respect. This means all job roles, all levels, all genders, all ethnicities, all ages. Everyone needs to believe they are respected.

Take Marriott International as an example, the hotel company that employs some 408,500 associates globally at its headquarters, regional offices, and managed properties. Founder Bill Marriott espoused the company's cornerstone credo that puts respect for employees at the center of their guiding philosophy: "If you take care of associates, they will take care of the customer."

In 2017, with a portfolio of 30 brands and over $17 billion in annual revenues, Marriott International was recognized as a FORTUNE 100 Best Company to Work For Legend, having been named to all 20 lists since they started being produced in 1998. When it comes to guiding principles, it looks like Bill Marriott chose a good one.

At the 2017 Great Place to Work For All conference, Marriott's CEO Arne Sorenson noted that society often places great value on higher-profile jobs, such as those in the tech sector, and the contributions of people in the service industry are often considered less dignified. Sorenson has a different belief. He believes that service jobs deserve "extraordinary dignity."[86] At Marriott, employees in service roles such as door attendants, front desk agents, and housekeepers are revered.

"The housekeepers are a group that I talk about most frequently," Sorenson said. "They are my heroes. They are usually women; they're often immigrants. They work extraordinarily hard. They come in and they do what is really selfless work, over and over. They do it for years, and they do it with pride."

At Marriott, service employees that are traditionally confined to the unseen "back of the house" are given a place of honor as the "heart of the house." With this slight turn of a phrase, thousands of employees are suddenly elevated to a place where they are both vital and visible—and a third dimension of the word "respect" comes into play, which is to "look back at, regard, consider." In any organization, a critical element of respect is that employees know they are seen, that their work matters…that *they* matter.

This level of respect—that is, truly holding each worker in high regard, and even deference—comes straight from the top at Marriott, and it lives up, down, and across the enterprise. As one associate from The Ritz-Carlton, a Marriott-owned brand, shared:

> I work in housekeeping, and we all treat each other as a family. We share each other's successes, pain, grief, and happiness. When someone is severely sick, has lost a loved one, and is going through severe personal crisis, we pull together, take a monetary collection, and share in the person's pain.
>
> I lost both of my parents in 2015. They died two months apart, and my superiors, colleagues, and peers helped to make an unbearable pain and my experiences more manageable. Recently, two of our members needed chemotherapy due to cancer, and two others held a company-wide raffle that yielded $4,000, which was divided between the two who had cancer.
>
> We are also treated with exemplary professionalism by management, and everyone treats each other with dignity and respect. We go out of our way to treat the guest in a special manner (above and beyond what is expected), and we support each other with dignity, humanity, and respect.
>
> The one thing that I would like to change to make this place a better place is myself. I'd like to speak better English and support my Ritz-Carlton family even better. I love my work, my coworkers, and our wonderful guests. This is the truth.
>
> —Employee, The Ritz-Carlton[87]

In this single associate's remarks, we can begin to see the impact that Marriott's leaders' beliefs have on literally thousands of lives. We also see the positive impact on the business, as the associate who is treated well wants to give the very best of herself back to the company. And it doesn't stop there.

Respect's Ripple Effect

Being respected on the job (or not) is ultimately about a feeling. It's the feeling people have about themselves and about their self-worth. This feeling has the remarkable power to transcend the workplace, rippling out to the farthest corners of our lives.

While positive experiences at work inspire high levels of self-esteem and confidence, as we have seen above, negative experiences can thwart our ability to thrive in the workplace. Even more disturbing, they can create a toxicity that spills over to other areas of life. Even small acts of disrespect can occupy our minds for days, as we replay the situation—and experience the associated negative feelings—again and again.[88]

Research also shows particularly egregious treatment from supervisors, such as being put down in front of others, can result in psychological distress and dissatisfaction with life. These actions have the tendency to "flow downhill" via displaced aggression, as employees vent their frustration on less-powerful family members at home.[89] This fact alone should be enough to give any manager pause the next time they feel like making someone feel small at work.

However, the sad truth is it's very common for employees to feel disrespected at work. A 2014 study of more than 20,000 employees around the world showed that *over half* (54 percent) experience a basic lack of respect from their leaders.[90]

On the flip side, the same study found employees who felt respected by leaders also reported 56 percent better health and well-being, and 89 percent greater enjoyment and satisfaction with their jobs. And, according to our research, employees who reported they were respected in key ways, such as being included in decisions that affect them, were 5.3 times more likely to experience a psychologically and emotionally healthy workplace.[91]

These results on employees' mental and physical well-being are critically important. Research from Stanford and Harvard Business Schools shows "health problems stemming from job stress, like hypertension, cardiovascular disease, and decreased mental health, can lead to fatal conditions that wind up killing about 120,000 people each year."[92] And as Paul Zak found in his studies on the neuroscience of trust, "Compared with people at low-trust companies, people at high-trust companies report: 74 percent less stress, 106 percent more energy at work, 50 percent higher productivity, 13 percent fewer sick days, 76 percent more engagement, 29 percent more satisfaction with their lives, 40 percent less burnout."[93]

Respecting an employee also means understanding they have commitments outside of work. When work and life commitments collide, employees, especially those who are caregivers, are at risk of tremendous levels of stress and overwhelm—a phenomenon that is only increasing. However, at the 100 Best Companies to Work For, 83 percent of employees say they are actively encouraged by their managers to balance their work and personal life, and 91 percent say they can take time off from work when they need to.[94]

Let's face it: through actions both big and small, leaders and managers wield enormous power over the general happiness, health, and well-being of their employees. If you're in this position, use your power for good by treating all of your employees with a high level of respect—in the true sense of the word. They'll thank you, their families will thank you, and your company will thank you too.

Empowering All to Achieve Their Personal Best

Beyond being treated with respect, another way that work "works" is when a person has opportunities to learn, grow, and shine.

This starts with organizations investing in employees' development. And in this regard, the Best Workplaces have led the way. While some organizations have cut learning and development budgets over the years amid recessions or for fear that their trained talent will jump ship, the 100 Best Companies to Work For have increased their commitment to boosting employees' skills.[95,96] The average company on the 1998 100 Best list offered employees approximately 35 hours per year of training. That number has grown to more than 58 hours for hourly employees and 65 hours for salaried—a 76 percent increase.

Enabling employees to progress professionally also means getting out of their way. It means giving them the freedom to flourish at work, without micromanagement. Here again, the Best Workplaces have improved. At the 100 Best Companies, the percentage of employees who say "management trusts people to do a good job without watching over their shoulders" has climbed 6 percent over the past two decades, to the point where nearly 9 in 10 employees experience a healthy level of autonomy.

This sense of autonomy is critical to the feeling of "flow" that humans long for—the state, sometimes called being "in the zone," when we lose ourselves in a task even as we find ourselves advancing our abilities.[97] The Best Workplaces recognize that this heightened state often involves working with others, who can challenge and teach us. Recall the Matrix Services employee quoted above who appreciated "a friendly environment" that was "conducive to learning," and the Synchrony Financial staffer who loves "coming to work and interacting with my team and other employees."

Working independently and interdependently, individuals at great workplaces often accomplish more than they thought possible. Just as amateur runners and other athletes love setting PRs (personal records), people at great workplaces are empowered to reach new heights professionally. Here's what one employee at the email marketing firm Return Path told us:

> I've had tremendous opportunity to grow my career here and contribute to the organization in a very meaningful way. I can honestly say that I've seen similar opportunities for many of my peers. If you step up to the challenge and take ownership, you are not limited in what you can achieve.

Opening the Doors Wider to Create Opportunities For All

Empowering people to become their best has great benefits for employees themselves but also for the company, as employees broaden and deepen their capabilities. However, this area presents unique challenges in building a Great Place to Work For All. Organizations often identify "high-potential" employees and focus development efforts on this group, or provide training only for certain roles that are more valued, such as managers or engineers.

And unfortunately, when it comes to demographic groups, the fact remains that some are more likely than others to be passed over for these opportunities, simply because they are female, or darker-skinned, or in a role that is not as valued. Research and direct testimonies from employees themselves continue to uncover many ways these groups are treated inequitably in the workplace, especially during performance reviews, promotions processes, and other career-advancing activities.

As a result, these employees are not well positioned for success, and they're less likely to achieve all they're capable of. Worse still, they lose out on advancement opportunities that put them in leadership positions, sending a clear message to employees who look like them that positions of power are not meant for them, furthering the inequity. We can see this at play by taking a simple look at the ranks of corporate America: 47 percent of the workforce are women but the same can be said of just 6.4 percent of FORTUNE 500 CEOs.[98]

Within science, engineering, and technology (SET) industries specifically, the Center for Talent Innovation reported that though approximately 80 to 90 percent of SET women love their work, a sizable proportion feel stalled and are likely to quit their jobs within a year. This is due in large part to workplace cultures that are exclusionary or even hostile to women, a scarcity of effective sponsors, and other barriers to leadership roles.[99]

The good news is, leaders at some of the best workplaces

are working harder to set a higher bar and overcome these challenges so all employees can thrive.

As an example, GoDaddy, the world's largest tech provider to small businesses and a recognized great workplace, conducted an in-depth examination, in partnership with Stanford's Clayman Institute for Gender Research, of the company's promotions and other advancement-related practices. The goal was to identify inequities. Driven by an unwavering belief that male and female employees deserve to be treated equitably, then-CEO Blake Irving was one of the forerunners in signing the Federal Equal-Pay Pledge and even wrote a book on the topic called *Decoding the Gender Bug.*[100]

Even still, GoDaddy found while pay was often fair between men and women at the company, there were hidden inequities across processes for selection, promotions, reviews, and rewards. For example, male engineers were promoted at a faster clip than women, and an audit of performance reviews showed that male engineers were measured on the quality of their code, while female engineers were more likely to be measured on "style" factors, such as how they worked on a team.

GoDaddy leaders have taken dramatic steps to improve. Immediate steps have included completely removing "style" as a measurement of success in the review process, and automatically flagging people based on how long they've been in their role, so people aren't required to "raise their hand" when they might be ready for promotion. As a result of these and other efforts, women and people of color are being promoted more effectively, and employees report a fairer experience of the workplace overall. They've also seen a decrease in voluntary turnover rates across the company—with the greatest improvement among women.[101]

Another example of offering opportunities more ubiquitously in the tech world comes from WP Engine, an Austin company and recognized Best Workplace that helps customers build and run websites on WordPress, the open source software. Here, the shared philosophy of "opening the door wider" drives recruitment and development efforts.

When CEO Heather Brunner joined WP Engine in 2013 and the company was taking off, she ended the practice of requiring job applicants to have a four-year college degree. It was a risky decision, since 69 percent of U.S. employers make college degrees mandatory for entry-level jobs, which presents a major barrier to entry for underprivileged, and often minority, swaths of the population.[102] Brunner wanted all people to have a chance at being part of the tech industry regardless of this requirement.

And it worked. In four years, WP Engine grew tenfold. Now, 5 percent of web users visit a WP Engine site every day, and the company is closing in on 100,000 customers in 140 countries around the globe. During the same time, the company has expanded its workforce to 475, of whom one-third don't have a college degree. New employees have come, in part, from coding academies and non-degree training programs.[103]

"We can let a lot more people come to the table and basically change the trajectory of their careers," Brunner says. "If you have the work ethic, if you match our culture, if you want to be a servant leader in terms of your style of how you work, and you're willing to come in and work hard and do the training that you need...we're willing to invest in you and bring people in. This has been game-changing for us."

The company also trains all employees to be financially literate and uses open book management. This starts in the new-hire orientation, where CFO April Downing teaches all new employees how to read the company's financials, what the key performance indicators are, and more. From then on, all employees receive monthly financial updates and have a clear understanding of how their efforts directly impact key metrics such as growth and customer retention.

"Young people [are] getting the light bulbs turned on around how their work impacts customer satisfaction and therefore customer satisfaction leads to an opportunity to retain, get advocacy, and grow," said Brunner.

By opening the doors wider and providing financial literacy training for all employees, WP Engine is creating opportunities for people who were otherwise blocked from the tech sector. In doing so, they're changing their small corner of the tech landscape. And as they boldly lead by example, they're paving the way for others to do the same.

Living a Life in Full Color

Opening the door wider allows workplaces to become rich communities that include people from more diverse backgrounds and varied walks of life. And the people we work with make up one of the most dominant communities in our lives. These relationships are real, and at many of the best workplaces, people report that their colleagues are akin to a second family. Though this feeling is not always the norm at work, it should be. As social creatures, having an authentic connection with the people we spend much of our waking lives with is something we need.

"I Can Be Myself Here"

Creating meaningful connections at work starts with welcoming all employees to bring their authentic selves to the table, every day. While employees at great workplaces have stated "I can be myself here" for decades, the idea of adopting an alter ego at work is becoming an increasingly unrealistic proposition. As more employees have public social media profiles and running online commentaries about their lives in and out of work, the boundaries between our "work" selves and our "real" selves are far fuzzier.

And this is a good thing. When people feel they can be themselves at work, they are experiencing psychological safety, which also allows them share their unique perspectives, their diverse experiences, and their most creative ideas—without fear of criticism that may otherwise stifle them.[104] This is good for business, as these elements clearly lead to more innovation and collaboration. On the spectrum of broader human development, it also lays the groundwork for enabling people to achieve their full potential, because they can "activate and interact in the world around them" in the most authentically meaningful ways.[105]

Beth Brooke-Marciniak, global vice chair of public policy at EY, a Big Four accounting firm and 100 Best Company to Work For, publicly shared what she believes is being left on the table when people can't be their authentic selves at work. Not only has Brooke-Marciniak been named nine times to the World's 100 Most Powerful Women list, but in 2011, she publicly came out as gay—and in that moment, became the most senior "out" female executive in the world.

At the Great Place to Work For All conference, she said, "I went from…living my life in what felt like in black and white, to life in full color. I had no idea how much the world and EY was not getting the best I had to offer. I would have argued with you five years earlier that they were getting everything I had to offer. I had no idea what was being left on the cutting room floor."[106]

Simply put, by creating an environment where employees can be themselves, they are positioned to be the very best they can be.

"I'm thankful that more of our employees in our workforces around the world are feeling free to be who they really are," said Brooke-Marciniak. "Nobody should have to live their life in black and white, because if they are, we're not getting the best of them."

The New Frontier of Care

Part of building authentic connections at work is caring for employees—both in and out of the workplace. While this includes encouraging work–life balance, it goes far beyond practices like giving employees a generous number of PTO (paid time off) days.

Rather, building a caring community at work means celebrating people during the good times and supporting them when the going gets tough. In fact, how a company supports its employees in times of need is a key indicator of a great workplace, which we have studied in depth as a part of identifying great workplaces around the world. Most of us will, at some time in our lives, face a major challenge that can be eased tremendously when our colleagues care, as illustrated earlier by the housekeeping associates at The Ritz-Carlton. In any strong community, when someone needs help, the troops rally around in support.

Some leaders are courageously bringing the concept of supporting employees in times of need into a new realm, because sometimes the support employees need isn't about money, or time off, or creating another HR policy. Sometimes, what's needed is to openly acknowledge and bear witness to an employee's—or group of employees'—experience.

And sometimes, that's the most difficult support to provide.

In July 2016, Tim Ryan was in his first week on the job as chairman of PwC when the national news was flooded with coverage of interracial police shootings in Dallas, Texas. In the wake of the tragedy and several preceding police-involved shootings of black men across the United States, Ryan shared that although leaders at his company knew employees were hurting, "the silence was deafening" when people showed up to work the next morning. "No one knew what to say," he said.[107]

In response, and against the advice of many of his peers and advisors, Ryan bravely decided to open up a company-wide dialogue about race that he knew would be uncomfortable but necessary. He framed the conversation to employees as "trying to gain an understanding of how we all feel; what it was like to be black in our country at that point in time; what it was like to be white, and trying to understand."

Once it began, the dialogue revealed powerful, previously unspoken truths facing PwC's black employees. For example, some colleagues shared that they felt safe when they were wearing a business suit to work. It served as a sort of superhero "cape" that, when removed after hours, left them vulnerable. Other colleagues shared that they taught their kids "how to get pulled over," keeping business cards in their front pockets to prove they were professionals who had purchased the cars they were driving.

So, this is real life. This is where the going gets tough, and it's where a forum for dialogue can help people. By having the conversation, employees' challenges and struggles are made known, and knowledge can lead to empathy. Knowledge can lead to support. And knowledge can lead to change.

Nancy Vitale, senior vice president of human resources at Genentech, noted how even small signs of support by way of dialogue can go a long way. A Muslim employee at Genentech shared with Vitale that her team member had simply asked her how she was doing, given some of the negative rhetoric about Muslims in the U.S., and wanted to know what they could do to support her. With tears streaming down her face, the woman shared that just having that question asked—how she was doing and what someone could do to help support her—made all the difference. "Those individual, one-on-one interactions are incredibly powerful," said Vitale.[108]

If we're talking about being authentic, and supporting employees through thick and thin, then we also need to start expanding what's traditionally been accepted as the way we support employees. Fortunately, change is afoot. Since 2016, Tim Ryan has secured the participation of more than 275 CEOs of some of the nation's largest corporations to join the "CEO Action for Diversity and Inclusion," where CEOs publicly pledge to create a safe workplace environment for dialogue, mitigate unconscious bias, and share best—and worst—practices.[109]

While the results of these efforts remain to be seen, the fact that these conversations are happening at the upper echelons of corporate America to this extent is a new and promising turn. The tides may just be turning toward a future where *all* employees who make up our workplace communities are fully supported and embraced.

Our Shared Quest for Meaning

In this chapter, we've looked at the many ways employees can be treated at work that will both honor and bring out the best of their human spirit.

The final topic in this chapter is not about how employees are treated but rather, whether they believe their work has meaning. Ultimately, all people—not just millennials—need to know their efforts make a difference in the world. Returning to Terkel's timeless observation: "Work is about a search for daily meaning as well as daily bread." The need for meaningful work is one that rings true across people and professions.

Indeed, the desire to feel connected to the outcome of our work appears to be hardwired into us. Most of us know this intuitively, because we feel it. The MIT Sloan School of Management found that even for futile tasks, such as identifying consecutive instances of the letter "s" on a piece of paper, people were more productive—and willing to repeat the task for incrementally less money—when they felt their work had meaning. In the case of matching the letter "s" the condition of "meaning" was simply that people were asked to write their name on the paper and were told their work would be examined by an experimenter and then placed into a file—as opposed to being ignored or shredded.[110]

This may be why, in our study of the 2016 FORTUNE 100 Best Companies to Work For, we found a striking connection between employees' intent to stay with their company "for a long time" and their belief that their "work has special meaning; this is more than 'just a job.'" Of the more than 50 factors associated with a great workplace (including fair pay and profit sharing, opportunities for professional development, special benefits and perks, a fun workplace, and much more), it was a sense of meaning and purpose that tracked *most* closely to employees' desire to stay with the company for the long term.[111]

The sky is the limit when it comes to ways to help foster this feeling among employees. At 100 Best Company W. L. Gore & Associates, the manufacturing company that invented Gore-Tex, associates gear up with the customers who use their technical fabrics, such as law enforcement and military professionals. This way, associates can hear feedback on the difference the product makes in the real-world environment in which it's used.[112] Or take outdoor retailer Recreational Equipment, Inc. (REI), whose mission is to "inspire, educate and outfit for a lifetime of outdoor adventure and stewardship." Despite being a retail environment, there are also programs that get employees outside, including classes employees deliver to customers to teach outdoors skills.[113]

The bottom line is that people, no matter their age or their role in the company, want and need to be connected to a sense of meaning at work. Whether it's a simple "thank you" from their manager or a shared vision about the company's reason for being, all employees should know that what they did that day at work meant something. Because, over time, a life filled with meaningful days at work equates to a lifetime of meaning.

Better For All

For most people in the world, the workplace lacks the elements that make us thrive as human beings—basic things like respect, opportunities for personal growth and achievement, a caring community, and a sense of meaning. However, by approaching each employee as a person who is worthy of all this, it is possible to create a work experience—and by extension, a life experience—that enables us to thrive. One employee at Schweitzer Engineering Laboratories summed it up perfectly:

> SEL values guide every individual employee-owner to pursue the vision of life and get closer to fulfilling that vision every day. Personally, at SEL, each day I contribute my best, I learn a lot, I get social with diverse people, I donate to help others. What else could be better in life than this?

So treat your employees well. It's better for them, and it's better for your business. And as we'll see in the next chapter, it's better for the world too.

Chapter 6
Better Business for a Better World

Great Places to Work For All help build a society defined by caring, fairness, shared prosperity, and individual opportunity.

As the U.S. space program was taking humanity to the moon last century, it was advancing our species on Earth as well. For one thing, NASA enabled African American women to play key roles in the "space race" against the Soviet Union.

The best-selling book (and hit movie) *Hidden Figures* captures the way African American women mathematicians, known as human "computers," helped crunch the numbers behind NASA's early rocket launches. One of the mathematicians, Katherine Johnson, calculated the complex trajectory for an orbital space flight. She got the assignment after asking for it boldly. "Tell me where you want the man to land," she said, "and I'll tell you where to send him up."[114]

She backed up the boldness with a 1960 research paper, the first report published by a woman from the Aerospace Mechanics Division at NASA's Langley Research Center. Johnson was so trusted that astronaut John Glenn asked for her to double-check the numbers from a mainframe computer before he lifted off on his historic flight to orbit the earth. Johnson also contributed to America's signature space achievement: putting a man on the moon. Johnson determined the exact time the lunar landing vehicle needed to leave the moon's surface to reconnect with the orbiting command service module.

NASA in those days was by no means a perfect place for women or African Americans. The 30 or so African American female "computers" depicted in the movie weren't treated fairly or treated with full respect—most of them worked in a segregated unit, expected to use "colored" bathrooms. But NASA's leaders wanted to achieve their mission. That meant they had to respect the mathematically powerful minds of those women to get the miraculous innovations required. And that respect, and the opportunities NASA provided, paid off for the women, the agency, and society. Although NASA's African American women were largely "hidden figures" for many years, their contributions are now widely known and appreciated. So not only did NASA's moonshots inspire people across the planet, Johnson and her peers gradually became important role models for both the African American community and for all girls and women interested in math and science.[115]

Despite its poor treatment of the African American "computers," NASA and its leadership came to play a positive role in creating a fairer society, particularly in the U.S. south.[116] Dr. Wernher von Braun, director of NASA's Marshall Space Flight Center in Huntsville, Alabama, spoke out against discrimination in a 1964 speech to local business leaders. Von Braun, an émigré from Germany considered the father of rocket technology, used an analogy from the Cold War in Europe to make the point that poll taxes and other voting restrictions were wrong. "All these regulatory barriers form a 'Berlin Wall' around the ballot box," he said. "I am not going to sit quietly on a major issue like segregation."[117]

More than 50 years after von Braun's comment, humanity still has not achieved full racial equality and inclusion. And globally, many other problems remain. Hundreds of millions of people spend the bulk of their time at workplaces that deaden their spirit, increase their stress, and erode their health. Thanks partly to frustrations with work, a lack of good jobs, and a tumultuous global economic system, the social fabric in the United States and around the globe is fraying. Political divides have widened as faith in each other has faltered.

In short, it's an urgent time for business leaders to decide what kind of workplace they want to lead and what kind of world they want to live in. Just as in von Braun's time, leaders have a choice about how to use their power and influence. Will they sit quietly in the face of challenges that seep into the business world? Or will they speak up and act—within and beyond their organizations—to solve problems plaguing society?

Today, leaders choosing the latter option are working to build Great Places to Work For All. These organizations are what the world needs now—desperately. By enabling people and businesses to reach their full potential, Great Places to Work For All help build a society defined by caring, fairness, shared prosperity, and individual opportunity.

Put another way, Great Places to Work For All free human beings everywhere to reach for the stars, as Katherine Johnson did, and to do so in harmony with one another.

In a World of Hurt

Harmony and mutual goodwill could use a boost today.

Suspicion and distrust are on the rise around the world. In 2017, the annual Trust Barometer published by communications firm Edelman showed that people's trust declined globally in the four key institutions of business, government, nonprofits, and the media. Edelman found a majority of respondents worldwide lack full faith that the "system" works for them. "In this climate, people's societal and economic concerns, including globalization, the pace of innovation and eroding social values, turn into fears, spurring the rise of populist actions now playing out in several Western-style democracies," Edelman concluded.[118]

A relatively free global economy has lifted millions out of poverty in the developing world over the past few decades.[119] But it has left behind many people in the developed world as jobs have moved overseas or been replaced by automation. The result has been heightened levels of financial insecurity, workplace stress, and increasing inequality within many developed nations.

Layoffs became a standard operating procedure in the 1990s and 2000s, and a whopping 8.7 million U.S. jobs were cut during the Great Recession roughly a decade ago.[120] Instability has continued during the subsequent recovery. Recent research by the Pew Charitable Trusts found nearly half of Americans regularly experienced substantial fluctuations in income, earnings increased just 2 percent over the past decade for the typical American family, and only half of Americans feel financially secure.[121]

Job insecurity is a key part of the job stress facing Americans. Also contributing to work-related anxiety are a faster pace of business, an always-on workplace culture, and growing challenges in meeting professional and personal commitments, including childcare and eldercare. The stress adds up to a little-discussed crisis, where work is literally killing us slow-ly.[122] As we mentioned in the previous chapter, work-related stress and the illnesses it causes lead to 120,000 deaths each year in America. That makes workplace anxiety more deadly than diabetes, Alzheimer's, or influenza.[123]

At the same time, the problem hits society in the pocket-book in the form of unnecessary health care costs. Jeffrey Pfef-fer, a Stanford University management professor and one of the authors of the research on the effects of workplace stress, esti-mates it costs the United States up to $190 billion annually—in-creasing the nation's health care costs by 5 to 8 percent.[124]

Rising Inequality Brings the World Down

Globally, income disparities have been declining amid the economic success of countries such as China and Brazil. But the global trade system has also led to growing levels of inequality within most developed nations.[125] That widening inequality represents a problem for individual countries and the world as a whole. Epidemiologist Richard Wilkinson has documented the corrosive effects on society when wealth disparities are large. Among them are physical and mental illness, violence, low math and literacy scores among young people, lower levels of trust, and weaker community life.[126]

These problems, he notes, stem from the way great in-equity in status leads human beings to see themselves as adversaries rather than allies. "Whether society has great inequality and a strong status hierarchy, whether there is a strong sense of superiority and inferiority, tells us whether we are in the same boat together and depend on cooperation and reciprocity, or whether we have to fend for ourselves in a dog-eat-dog society," Wilkinson writes.

It also turns out that our overall global prosperity suffers from high levels of inequality. A 2014 study by the Organization for Economic Cooperation and Development found that countries where income inequality is decreasing grow faster than those with rising inequality.[127]

Not only is our world facing challenges of inequality, job stress, economic insecurity, and distrust, but the human race is pining for a good job. That's what polling firm Gallup found in its surveys of global sentiment. Over the last century, the "will of the world" changed from wanting things such as peace, freedom, and family to wanting a good job.[128] This shift is driven in part by young people who forge close friendships through work and want meaning and development from their jobs, says Gallup CEO Jim Clifton. And yet, as we mentioned in the previous chapter, Gallup also has discovered that just 30 percent of Americans are engaged at work, a number that drops to a paltry 15 percent worldwide.

"What the whole world wants is a good job, and we are failing to deliver it—particularly to millennials," Clifton says. "This means human development is failing, too. Most millennials are coming to work with great enthusiasm, but the old management practices—forms, [focusing on skill] gaps, and annual reviews—grinds the life out of them."[129]

The Role of Great Places to Work For All

We agree with Clifton overall. We waste human potential at workplaces worldwide on a scale that is scarcely imaginable.

Charging Up Safety at Work

An estimated 1,000 people die at work each day. But Elektro Eletricidade e Serviços is standing up for safety.

The 3,700-employee Brazilian electrical utility company experienced roughly 12 accidents annually in the late 2000s, including two deaths. The checkered safety record reflected the company's priorities: it focused investments on technology rather than employees. But under Marcio Fernandes, who became president in 2011, Elektro became a Brazilian power industry leader in embracing a "Zero-Accident" vision. It aimed to reduce annual workplace injuries to zero and adopted a data-driven, behavior-based training program for safety.

"For many years we were focused on investing in machines," Fernandes says. "After this, we decided to invest strongly in the people."

Since 2011 there have been no workplace deaths. In 2014, Elektro reported just three accidents causing employees to miss a day or more of work; this dropped to zero in 2015 and one in 2016.

Great safety has accompanied better business results. From 2012 to 2016, Elektro enjoyed a 10 percent jump in a key earnings measure. Also in 2016, it won an industry award for superior customer service. Fernandes calls Elektro's human-centric, profitable surge in recent years a "double success."

But not all companies are failing to deliver a good job or promote human development. The best workplaces, the ones we've honored on our lists and that are striving to become Great Places to Work For All, are delivering these goods and more. They are quietly counteracting global trends of mistrust, economic anxiety, and inequality.

They provide not only good jobs but great ones. Not just

full-time work with a steady paycheck but a workplace where people trust their leaders, enjoy their colleagues, and take pride in their jobs. What's more, these workplaces have been getting better over time. We have noted that even the best workplaces have gaps—pockets of people not having as positive an experience as others. Still, the overall levels of trust, pride, and camaraderie that we measure in our employee surveys have climbed 14 percent over the 20 years we've been ranking the 100 Best Companies to Work For in America. In 2017, a striking 91 percent of employees at the 100 Best said that taking everything into account, they would call their organization a great place to work.

And those great experiences ripple outward.

Companies that Care

In the first place, Great Places to Work For All contribute to a world that's more caring. This starts with the ways these organizations foster positive, human relationships at work, where leaders and coworkers care about each other. People aren't cogs in a machine, mere numbers, or warm bodies. As we discussed in the previous chapter, coworkers facing crises like a serious illness or the death of a loved one can expect support, concern, consoling.

But the care employees experience at a great workplace comes from more than just the empathy of bosses and colleagues. Among the factors that Stanford's Jeffrey Pfeffer cites for a healthy environment that minimizes stress-related illnesses are a measure of control over one's work, the ability to resolve conflicts between work and family commitments, perceived justice at work, and job security. All these are generally present at Great Places to Work For All. For example, even as many Americans have ridden an economic roller coaster that's left them more anxious than thrilled, the Best Workplaces have preserved—or increased—a measure of job stability. The share of employees at the 100 Best who say "I believe management would lay people off only as a last resort" has ticked upward, from 81 percent in 1998 to 85 percent in 2017.

It adds up to a holistically healthier environment. At the 2017 100 Best Companies, 84 percent said they work at a "psychologically and emotionally healthy place to work." In other words, people generally don't experience the lingering feelings of anger and humiliation from being ridiculed by the boss. They don't worry about leaving work early to see a child's soccer game. In fact, many have some level of control over their hours and where they work. And they don't feel powerless about how to do their job well or worry that their position will be wiped out on a whim. On the contrary, they feel respected. For the most part, they feel great at work.

And they bring that positivity home, where they can be better at caring for the people in their lives beyond work: their spouses or partners, their kids, their friends and neighbors.

As one employee at a Great Place to Work–Certified company shared:

> What REALLY works for me is my full-time work from home status. I LOVE this benefit more than anything else. I'm able to have three hours back in my day that I would otherwise spend on getting ready and commuting. Instead, I use this time to exercise and get dinner on the table for my kids at a reasonable time! I am a better employee, a better wife, and a better mom because of this benefit and for that I am extremely grateful.

Many great workplaces take care a step further, with generous policies that enable and help employees to care for family members in need. In 2016, for example, professional services firm Deloitte announced it would give employees 16 weeks of fully paid family leave time for caregiving. The benefit is very generous by U.S. standards, where companies are not required by federal law to give employees paid time off.[130]

Health insurance coverage is another way great workplaces care for a wider circle of people. As a rule, the 100 Best offer coverage for employees and their family members. And amidst turmoil about the fate of federal policy on health care, employer-provided health insurance is the most desired employment benefit.[131]

Apart from directly providing support to employees and their loved ones, great workplaces typically show significant care for the communities around them.[132] Much of the community service by great workplaces takes place locally, but many organizations extend their care across the globe. Belgian shoe store chain Torfs is a good example. The 600-employee company, a Best Workplace in Europe, has supported disadvantaged children in poorer countries, including a group of students in Nepal. Torfs employees effectively adopted these 31 children, with some staffers traveling to the Nepalese village of Sekha to work directly with community leaders.

When Nepal suffered a massive earthquake in April 2015, it shook Torfs employees half a world away. They organized a fundraising campaign at stores. Isabel Van Goethem, a marketing employee at Torfs, wrote a blog on the company website about how her own children were anxious to hear about whether one of the Torfs's "godchildren" in Nepal, Nikesh, was okay in the wake of the earthquake. "The devastation is enormous, we see the images on the news but also the pictures that we see from our Nepalese friends," Van Goethem wrote. "My heart sinks into my shoes."

Hearts lightened some as Torfs employees learned that the Nepalese children they have bonded with in Sekha survived the big quake and aftershocks. The incident captures the way the Great Places to Work For All build a more caring world in concentric circles. Employees, family members, and people in communities near and far connect, look after each other, treat each other better.

Fairness on the March

Great Places to Work For All have a similar impact regarding fairness—the second major way they contribute to a better world.

This fairness effect begins with a devotion on the part of leaders at Great Places to Work For All to treat people equitably. Fairness is a simple concept, but it is not easy for leaders to achieve—especially in large, complex organizations. Fair treatment in pay, promotions, and other matters isn't necessarily equal treatment, given different job levels and responsibilities.

Nonetheless, the Best Workplaces have made significant progress over the past 20 years when it comes to evenhandedness. Employee ratings of fairness have improved 22 percent at the 100 Best from 1998 to 2017, outpacing the other four workplace dimensions we measure—respect, credibility, pride, and camaraderie.

Best Workplaces have been at the forefront of pushing to

close gender pay gaps. These efforts are part of a larger picture showing great workplaces to be countering the income disparities that can be so corrosive in society. To be sure, the CEOs of Best Workplaces earn pay packages that can reach into the millions. But these organizations demonstrate a measure of restraint in their executive pay often lacking at other big companies. In a 2016 study with research firm Equilar, we found the median CEO pay at publicly traded 100 Best Companies was about 19 percent less than at the S&P 500 ($8.3 million vs. $10.3 million).[133] In other words, CEOs at great workplaces are paid plenty, but they are more concerned than their peers elsewhere about sharing the gains with their entire team.

Indeed, employee perceptions that they are paid fairly has risen over the past 20 years at the 100 Best. The figure has climbed 22 percent, such that in 2017, nearly four out of five employees believed pay was fair.

Beyond greater economic fairness, great workplaces are promoting a society that treats all its members equitably. Yes, within the walls of great workplaces, there are groups not having as positive an experience as others. But the Best Workplaces have been making progress. For example, the share of employees who say people are treated fairly regardless of race has climbed 10 percentage points to 95 percent, while belief in equitable treatment regardless of gender has jumped 12 percentage points to 93 percent. We didn't track bias against employees identifying as LGBTQ in 1998, but in 2017, fully 96 percent of employees at the 100 Best said people were treated fairly regardless of their sexual orientation. And as we've discussed earlier, leaders of Best Workplaces, such as EY's Beth Brooke-Marciniak and PwC's Tim Ryan, are raising their voices in the public sphere, calling explicitly for a more inclusive, kinder, fairer society.

Great Places to Work For All, though, aren't just fostering greater fairness in the United States. The impact is global. Marriott's expansion into India in 2001 is a good example. Most Indian hotels at the time expected employees to work six days a week. Marriott bucked that trend with a workweek expectation closer to what its employees in the developed world experienced. The company established a five-and-a-half-day workweek, meaning that staffers would take two days off every second week.

Rajeev Menon, Marriott's chief operating officer for the Asia Pacific region (excluding Greater China), recalls that the decision caused an "uproar" in the hospitality field, with some industry leaders calling it an unsustainably generous policy toward employees. But Marriott stuck to its "People First" philosophy—that by taking great care of their employees, the employees will take great care of customers. That enlightened ethos has only fueled the company's progress in South Asia—defined as India, Sri Lanka, Bangladesh, the Maldives, and Nepal. Over the past 11 years, Marriott opened 8 hotels in the region with another 17 planned in the next few years.[134] And rivals have reversed course on the shorter workweek. "Now a number of our competitors have followed our lead," Menon says.

Not only did Marriott lift labor standards in India, but it took aim at a privilege of the business elite. The company refused to go along with a tradition in the India hospitality industry whereby rank-and-file staff members ate in one cafeteria while hotel executives enjoyed a separate, exclusive dining room. "We said we're going to have one associate dining room, for everyone from general managers to frontline associates," Menon recalls.

This is what a fairer world looks like. Where working-class Indian housekeepers are breaking bread with business leaders. Where people who've long felt excluded based on their racial or gender or sexual orientation are invited to the table. Where people are compensated in an equitable way.

While much of the world sees a playing field tilted in favor of the powerful, great workplaces are working to level it—for the benefit of all.

A Bigger, Shared Pie

A fairer world relates to the third major way Great Places to Work For All are making the world better: through shared prosperity.

We just discussed equitable pay practices. But we're not only talking about how the pie is sliced and distributed. We're talking about making the pie bigger—much bigger. As we've seen, high-trust workplaces grow fast, and For All cultures accelerate that growth. If you recall from Chapter 1, companies in the top quartile on our For All Score enjoy more than three times the revenue growth of companies in the bottom quartile.

You might argue that fast-growing companies do not signal more prosperity for a country or the world as a whole. After all, the success of one business can spell the demise of another and the loss of jobs. But the key ingredient of great workplaces—trust—has been shown to be a kind of economic tonic on a grand scale. Great workplaces depend on leaders and rank-and-file employees developing trusting relationships. As we saw with caring for people, developing a mindset of trusting others tends to spill out beyond the workplace. People at these organizations begin to have more faith in others in their broader communities. And it is precisely when societies have "high-radius trust"—when even strangers tend to give each other the benefit of the doubt—that economic performance improves on a national level.[135] Nobel Prize–winning economist Kenneth Arrow put it this way: "Virtually every commercial transaction has within itself an element of trust, certainly any transaction conducted over a period of time. It can be plausibly argued that much of the economic backwardness in the world can be explained by the lack of mutual confidence."[136]

Companies alone cannot ensure that all people in a nation or worldwide share in economic progress, especially during turbulent times. But we see the Best Workplaces doing something critical that helps their people at least prepare for downturns and changes: training employees. As noted earlier, the average company on the 1998 Best 100 list offered employees approximately 35 hours per year of training and development. That number has grown to more than 58 hours for hourly employees and 65 hours for salaried workers.

AT&T's massive effort to retrain its workforce is a sign of the way the Best Workplaces are helping their people remain valuable contributors. CEO Randall Stephenson portrays the training offer as a broader economic pact. "It's a new contract, a societal contract," Stephenson says. "The world is changing and it's changing fast. If you are interested in keeping up, we're going to give you the tools and everything you need to equip yourself for the future."

Great Places to Work encourage a sense of shared prosperity beyond money alone. They help growing numbers of people feel they are sharing in the good life. To illustrate this point, look at Liderman, a Peruvian company that provides security services. Most Liderman employees are security guards, earning salaries of about $400 per month, often living in poor neighborhoods in Lima. Liderman leaders took note of the fact that many of its employees live in homes without decent bathrooms, where they and their families have what amount to outhouses or crude, unpleasant toilets. The company made it a policy to give employees interest-free loans to renovate their homes, often in the form of better bathrooms. Liderman employees take such pride in their company-assisted upgrades that many post "before" and "after" photos of the projects online.

A nice bathroom is an important sign of sharing in modern comforts. In effect, Liderman is helping people of modest means, in jobs—security guard roles—that historically haven't come with much prestige, to share in the dignity that economic progress and prosperity have provided the human race.

Today's global economy often leaves some to sink. But Great Places to Work For All are lifting all boats.

Empowering Individuals

Just as they promote shared prosperity, Great Places to Work For All also advance economic opportunity and empowerment around the globe. This is the fourth way these workplaces make the world a better place. People generally want the ability to improve their economic lot in life, and parents have long hoped that their children could do better than the prior

generation. But amid growing wealth disparities, many people are skeptical about economic mobility; nearly two-thirds
of people in advanced economies think that children will be
worse off than their parents.[137] Barriers to individual progress and decreased faith in the economic system help widen
the social fissures within countries and globally, but the Best
Workplaces are countering the trend. They are freeing people
to move forward, empowering them economically.

This happens in part through the extensive training commitments we've discussed. Another example along these lines
is Elektro Eletricidade e Serviços, a Brazilian electric utility
company. When Marcio Fernandes became president of Elektro in 2011, he juiced up professional development investments
in the form of new career paths and training options.

Tiago and Josiane Souza, a married couple who are both
electricians at Elektro, jumped at the chance to elevate their
careers. Both enrolled in an electrical engineering program
at a local university. Josiane made the leap into college after
noticing that Elektro colleagues were progressing from the
position of electrician to electrical engineer—with the company's support. "Elektro inspired me to go after a college degree," she says. "I never thought I would get one. I saw that if a
person studies, they have the opportunity to grow in the company." Earning an engineering degree will mark a milestone
not just for Josiane and Tiago but for their families—none of
their parents attended college.

Another form of economic empowerment is the ability to
control your destiny at work. To have a measure of autonomy
over how you do your job and a say in workplace decisions.
In the last chapter, we noted that the 100 Best have reduced

micromanagement over the past two decades. It's also true that workplace democracy has improved at these companies. In 1998, just 64 percent of employees said management involved people in decisions that affect their jobs. That figure had jumped to 77 percent in 2017. The rise in the share of employees at the 100 Best who say leaders genuinely seek and respond to employee suggestions is nearly as impressive. It's a 19 percent increase, to the point where 82 percent of employees at the 100 Best now feel their ideas matter.

One of the companies that most empowers employees at work is manufacturer W. L. Gore & Associates. One of Gore's guiding principles is freedom: "We encourage each other to grow in knowledge, skill, scope of responsibility and range of activities. We believe that Associates will exceed expectations when given the freedom to do so." Another is commitment: "We are not assigned tasks; rather, we each make our own commitments and keep them." In keeping with these values, Gore allows employees to form their teams based on the ability of individual employees to recruit peers to a compelling project. Gore also lets employees rank colleagues on their contributions to the company—a ranking that helps determine salary raises.

Among the Gore employees who have benefited from freedom at work is Monika Fattorello, a human resources professional for Gore in Italy. Fattorello has been able to pursue her passions in communication and training. So besides handling HR tasks for Gore's associates in Italy, Fattorello also has taught courses in communication skills—such as how leaders can give effective feedback—to Gore colleagues in Italy, Spain, and other countries in Europe.

Her experience at Gore has been a radical departure from what she'd experienced at her three previous workplaces. At former employers, managers tended to view her as requiring close scrutiny and as fundamentally flawed. "Before the end of the day, I'd have to tell someone what I'd done, and they'd tell me what I'd done wrong," she says. "My leaders at Gore trust me."

Working on a Solution

We've seen how Great Places to Work For All are combating global problems like mistrust, economic anxiety, and a lack of opportunity. In effect, they are strengthening the social fabric. Against a backdrop of widening differences, the Best Workplaces have been fostering greater social cohesion. Consider how these measures of collegiality, caring, and solidarity have increased at the 100 Best over the past 20 years (see Figure 18). In each of the categories related to workplace harmony, the 100 Best as a whole have seen employee scores improve at least 10 percent.

The 100 Best represent a fraction of the U.S. workforce. But not a tiny one: the 2017 FORTUNE 100 Best employed a total of 2.3 million people. What's more, we're not talking about small, local businesses where everyone can get to know one another easily. We're talking about large organizations, such as Cisco, Genentech, PwC, and Salesforce, that are national and even global in scope. Whole Foods Market, Marriott, and Edward Jones have operations in 40 or more U.S. states. The Best Companies have managed to foster friendships and caring connections across blue and red states, with employees of

Figure 18

Best Workplaces
Strengthen Society

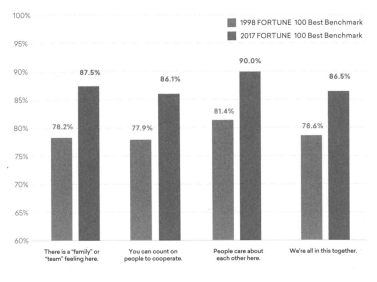

Source: Great Place to Work analysis

different races, nationalities, and religions, among employees in both the C-suite and the boiler room.

And in just the past couple of years, leaders of Best Workplaces have been stepping up to play larger public roles, speaking out in favor of a more unified, inclusive society. They are answering a call issued in the Edelman report on rising suspicions globally: "To rebuild trust and restore faith in the system, institutions must step outside of their traditional roles and work toward a new, more integrated operating model that puts people—and the addressing of their fears—at the center of everything they do."[138]

Elevating Everyone

Might the Best Workplaces be doing more than healing a world that's hurting? Could Great Places to Work For All have the potential to elevate the human race? Raise our consciousness?

Author Frederic Laloux's book *Reinventing Organizations* makes the case that a new level of human consciousness is emerging, as is a corresponding new, "more soulful" nonhierarchical approach to organizations. Laloux, a former management consultant, argues that traditional, top-down companies have killed our spirits and threatened our viability as a species with their focus on unbridled growth. But he sees a different breed of organization taking shape, one that parallels a stage in human development labeled "Teal." It is in keeping with psychologist Abraham Maslow's highest stage of "self-actualization" and involves letting go of ego and fear—in favor of trust. "All wisdom traditions posit the profound truth that there are two fundamental ways to live life: from fear and scarcity or from trust and abundance," Laloux writes.[139]

Laloux's suggestion that organizations are moving in a healthy, humanistic direction dovetails with other social theorists who see the course of human history heading toward greater cooperation.[140] If so, Great Places to Work For All are on the right side of history. With many decentralized, purposeful, community "Teal" features, these organizations are serving as engines to elevate the human spirit.

A Lever to Move the World

It would be going too far to call NASA in the 1960s a Great Place to Work For All. But the agency played a role in expanding opportunities on Earth even as its missions into space fired up imaginations and united much of the planet. People worldwide were pulling for the Apollo astronauts and thrilled when Neil Armstrong took humankind's first step onto the moon in 1969. Katherine Johnson, whose calculations helped make that small-yet-giant step possible, was among those enthralled by the moment. The level of respect she experienced at NASA, combined with the challenges of her work and the epic purpose of pushing beyond Earth's boundaries, made her job a joy.

"I loved every single day of it," Johnson said of her 33-year career. "There wasn't one day when I didn't wake up excited to go to work."[141]

Unfortunately, most people today do not feel the same way about their jobs. Work is a place where people generally feel stuck, stressed, and deadened, where seeds of division are sown. But when you think about it, what better lever is there to lift us up as a species? Work is where people spend the lion's share of their waking hours. What if every day, everyone had the kind of caring, fair, purposeful, stimulating experience that people at great workplaces have? The kind of human beings shaped by those organizations could potentially solve our seemingly intractable problems: sectarian struggles, armed conflicts, continuing poverty, challenging diseases. We could reach our potential as a human race.

In essence, this is our mission at Great Place to Work. We are working to build a better world by helping organizations become Great Places to Work For All. To do so, we need leaders to join us. Leaders willing and able to create a great experience for everyone, no matter who they are or what they do for the company.

We call this kind of a leader a For All Leader, and in the next chapter we lay out our new research into how to become one.

Part Three

The For All Leadership Call

Chapter 7

Leading to a Great Place to Work For All

We define the key leadership behaviors for building a Great Place to Work For All, based on our newest research on effective leadership.

Who Is the For All Leader?

So far, the chapters in this book have presented a composite For All "super leader." Someone who leads with the humility of NBA champs Steve Kerr and Steph Curry, and with the authenticity of EY's Beth Brooke-Marciniak—one of the most senior "out" executives in the world. A leader who has the agility to navigate an organization of more than 260,000 employees into the future of technology, like AT&T's Randall Stephenson. A leader who has the courage to say what's never been said before in the workplace about race—and inspire others to do the same—like Tim Ryan of PwC. A leader who is willing to spend $6 million (and counting) to create a fairer workplace by balancing pay inequities, like Marc Benioff at Salesforce. Who leads with dignity and respect for each employee, like Marriott International CEO Arne Sorenson. A leader who is willing to tear down the status quo to open the doors wider in the tech industry, like WP Engine CEO Heather Brunner.

A For All Leader is someone who looks to employees across the company for the next great idea; who leads with values first, especially in the face of adversity. One who builds connectivity within and across teams; who can help inspire a sense of purpose and pride in employees; who elevates employees to achieve all they ever thought they were capable of, and then some.

We admit, it's a tall order.

While these examples are lofty, they shine a light on what's possible, on the fundamental qualities leaders need to navigate the emerging business landscape. In the new world of work, transparency trumps backroom deals, connectivity and care trump a "me first" attitude, and purpose trumps profit. Human potential is the name of the game, fairness is the playbook, and the companies that are most inclusive win.

And, the good news is, everyone can play, regardless of their company's size or industry. Mayvenn, Inc., which offers a mobile platform that allows stylists to sell hair extensions, was recognized as one of the Best Small and Medium Workplaces in the San Francisco Bay Area. Their CEO, Diishan Imira, started this mission-driven company with the goal of bringing some of the profit from the multibillion-dollar hair extension industry back into the pockets of the community that purchases them.

Imira said, "Hairstylists are some of the most important people we have. I want to give them the recognition they deserve. As of mid-July of 2017 we have created 55,000 new entrepreneurs whose fastest-growing revenue source comes from us." With guiding commitments such as to "value all of our customers, and invest in our community," fully 100 percent of Mayvenn's 38 employees say the company is a great place to work.[142]

Or, look at GoFundMe, an online fundraising company and recognized Best Workplace, where 100% of their 143 employees report that it is a great place to work.[143] Here, CEO Ron Soloman is "driven to make a real, meaningful impact in the world, leveraging technology and human compassion to lend a helping hand."[144]

These one-off examples may seem inconsequential, but collectively, small companies pack an enormous punch on the broader scale of U.S. business and the corresponding human experience of work. Small companies (companies with fewer than 500 employees) make up fully 99.7 percent of employer firms in the U.S., and they employ nearly half of the nation's workforce.[145] It's critical that leaders from businesses of all profiles understand that the For All ideals apply to them. Being a leader of a great workplace is not a function of your company's size or resources. It's a function of how you treat the people who work there. And as we've seen, there is a clear business case for treating those people well. When leaders are more inclusive, more inspiring, and more caring, they win on outcomes like talent retention, innovation, and revenue growth. As mentioned earlier, we found when employees in a high-trust culture experienced a caring workplace, they were 44 percent more likely to work for a company with above-average revenue growth.[146] There are hard-nosed business reasons for taking the "soft stuff" seriously.

The data is in, and it's in everyone's best interest for leaders to take a close look at themselves and see how they measure up against the new standard—the For All standard.

The For All Leadership Model

We've shared that just 15 percent of the world's one billion full-time workers are engaged at work. As Jim Clifton, chairman and CEO of Gallup, astutely noted, "Employees everywhere don't necessarily hate the company or organization they work for as much as they do their boss. Employees—especially the stars—join a company and then quit their manager."[147]

A Great Place to Work For All must have great managers for all. As described in Chapter 3, the ubiquitous presence of great managers at a company relies on a diverse executive team that models how to build meaningful human connections while executing business operations and analytics. With an effective leadership team at the helm, managers throughout the company are better equipped to foster a great place to work for all their employees.

But what are the day-to-day leadership practices that will make it happen? To understand how managers are leading their teams to a Great Place to Work For All, we dug into our data from hundreds of companies over many years. Our analysis covered a robust sample of 75,000 employees and more than 10,000 managers working primarily in the U.S., across industries including retail, hospitality, manufacturing, technology, finance, and health care. We reviewed employees' ratings of their workplaces as well as their open-ended comments about their managers. In analyzing the data, we looked for patterns and traits distinguishing great leaders from the not-so-great.

Based on those employee evaluations and comments, we identified five distinct leadership levels, which we've characterized into personas based on prominent themes.

> Level 1: The Unintentional Leader
> Level 2: The Hit-or-Miss Leader

> Level 3: The Transactional Leader
> Level 4: The Good Leader
> Level 5: The For All Leader

Together, they represent the For All Leadership Model. With each leadership level, a higher percentage of employees report they consistently experience a great workplace. Moving from level to level, we also found a corresponding improvement in the areas of innovation, productivity, employee retention, and organizational agility.

Our research shows that while For All Leaders surpass other leaders across all areas of trust, pride, and camaraderie in the workplace, the most dramatic differences are:

> Working with teams, including seeking out peoples' input and involving them in decisions
> Recognizing people, from calling out their accomplishments to helping them get ahead in their careers
> Being someone people want to follow because they are confident that the leader is competent, honest, and reliable

In these three areas, the differences our research uncovered between the best and the worst leaders are remarkable. Employees who identify their managers as For All Leaders are up to eight times more likely to give them high ratings in the areas noted above, compared to employees with managers at the lowest level.

Results across retention, productivity, innovation, and agility increased incrementally across all five levels as well. When comparing employees with a Level 1 Unintentional

Figure 19

Leaders Who Level Up Get Results

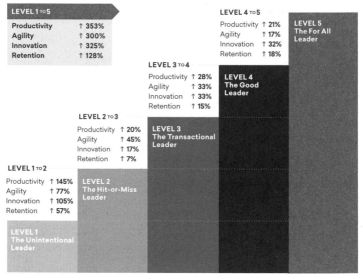

Source: Great Place to Work analysis

Leader to employees with a Level 5 For All Leader, the improvement is particularly dramatic. Employees with a For All Leader demonstrated:

- 353 percent higher productivity
- 300 percent greater agility
- 325 percent greater readiness to innovate
- 128 percent greater desire to stay

While not all leaders are necessarily able to evolve from Unintentional to For All, a jump from one level to the next is worth the effort. Even incremental improvements have a broad positive impact on the company and the people who

Figure 20

The For All Leadership Model

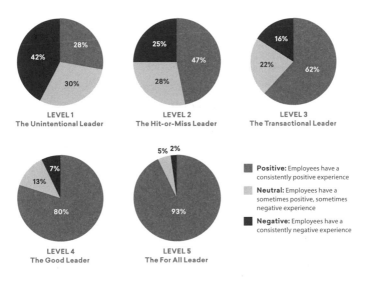

LEVEL 1
The Unintentional Leader

LEVEL 2
The Hit-or-Miss Leader

LEVEL 3
The Transactional Leader

LEVEL 4
The Good Leader

LEVEL 5
The For All Leader

Positive: Employees have a consistently positive experience

Neutral: Employees have a sometimes positive, sometimes negative experience

Negative: Employees have a consistently negative experience

Source: Great Place to Work analysis

work there. For example, employees with a Level 2 leader are 60 percent more likely to have a positive experience of the workplace than those with a Level 1 leader. They also demonstrate a 105 percent increase in innovation and a 145 percent improvement in productivity. Figure 19 shows the improvement in these areas moving from level to level.

When we put these results into the context of each of the five leadership personas, the reasons for these differences become clear.

The pie charts in Figure 20 show the percentages of employees who reported they have a positive experience of their manager, their teams, and of the workplace overall, broken out by what type of leader they have.

In all five charts:

> **Blue** represents the percentage of employees who report a consistently positive experience of their manager, their teams, and the workplace overall. Under the For All Leader, 93 percent of employees report they consistently experience a great workplace; this number falls to just 28 percent across employees whose boss is the Unintentional Leader.

> **Gray** represents the percentage of employees who report a sometimes positive and sometimes negative experience. Under the For All Leader, just 5 percent of employees report this relatively neutral experience; under the Unintentional Leader this jumps to 30 percent.

> **Black** represents the percentage of employees who report a consistently negative experience of the workplace. Under the Unintentional Leader 42 percent of employees have a negative experience of their manager, their teams, and the workplace overall; under the For All Leader, this falls to a mere 2 percent.

Looking across the charts, it's easy to see what we mean by the For All Leader. More than 9 in 10 employees with these leaders experience a great place to work, nearly all the time. Within these teams, it is a great place to work—for all.

Charting the Leadership Journey

Now we'll take a deeper dive into each persona, examining how the different leadership styles affect the people and organizations they work with. By looking at the specific behaviors associated with each type of leader, we can see what changes would enable the leader to move up to the next level.

Level 1: The Unintentional Leader

Common employee experience:

"I don't get paid enough to put up with this!"

The Unintentional Leader is easy to spot. These are leaders who don't seem conscious of the impact they have on others, so their behavior can hurt the people they work with and the organization. They often fail to inspire confidence. Employees reporting to an Unintentional Leader might feel like passengers on a bus whose driver doesn't have a destination in mind and doesn't tell the passengers what's going on.

Nobody sets out to be an Unintentional Leader. People end up that way for various reasons, including some not entirely of their own making. They may have been so great at their job, they were promoted to supervise people doing the same type of work—and then not given the training needed to lead. They could have amazing technical skills but lack the people skills a leader needs to inspire and motivate. They could be dealing with a health issue, addiction, family crisis, or other personal problem that hinders their ability to bring their best self to work. They may mistakenly believe that being a leader means acting like a drill sergeant: barking orders, and keeping their compassion and humanity under wraps.

"I am not saying that she is a horrible manager," one employee says of their Unintentional Leader. "All I am saying is that she needs to relax a little sometimes and talk to us without yelling or being so mad." Another says, "When I have asked a question or brought up a concern, [my manager] makes me feel like an idiot for asking."[148]

As you can expect, employees find working for an Unintentional Leader demoralizing, a circumstance that affects productivity, teamwork, and turnover. According to our research, close to three quarters (72 percent) of people who work for an Unintentional Leader do not consistently have a positive experience of work. As compared to the teams of Level 2 leaders, teams reporting to Level 1 leaders are 59 percent less likely to go above and beyond what is required of them on the job. They are also 36 percent less likely than employees working for Level 2 leaders to say they want to stay in their current job. Keeping an Unintentional Leader on staff hurts an organization's finances in the long run as the higher voluntary turnover (especially among top talent) directly affects the bottom line.

Think back to the example of Uber, whose former CEO was caught on tape cursing out an Uber driver, and his company's documented lack of regard for female engineers' claims of sexual harassment. The damage done not only to these employees but also to the company overall was devastating, as hundreds of thousands of customers joined the #DeleteUber movement once these and other events became public. Ultimately, based on these and other egregious leadership errors, the board of directors realized that Kalanick could not stay on as CEO without doing further damage to the company he had founded.

You might be an Unintentional Leader if you...
  » Think in terms of "employees" versus "people" who have full, complex lives

> Take credit for work you didn't do
> Withhold information from direct reports
> Are too consumed with worries about personal matters to care about the job
> Have not made changes after receiving negative people-related performance review feedback
> Reveal your frustrations by raising your voice or being personal in your criticism of others

Leveling Up

The news for the Unintentional Leader isn't all bad. Small changes can result in enough improvement to move up to the next level—with great positive impact for the company and its employees. Such changes could include getting proper training, acting in a more approachable manner, or making an effort to collaborate with employees more often. Adopting a more open, accepting attitude could dissolve employees' fears and animosities, which could in turn improve their confidence in their manager's abilities. It could also help break up the toxic environment, allowing people to focus less on getting through the day and more on the task at hand, making it less likely they would want to find another job.

However, there's only so far an organization should go. Even if an Unintentional Leader is also a star performer, keeping someone like this in a leadership role is bad for business. In the long run, a company is better off offering them a short window to do better—a 30-day probationary period, for example—and parting ways or removing leadership responsibilities if they don't improve.

Level 2: The Hit-or-Miss Leader

Common employee experience:

"Anybody home?"

The Hit-or-Miss Leader isn't terrible—at least not all of the time, and not for everyone they work with. That's the thing about this type of leader—they're on or off, hot or cold, a good friend or ally to some but not to others. Unlike an Unintentional Leader, they don't actively hurt an organization, but neither are they actively supporting their team or performing their duties to the extent the organization needs. A Hit-or-Miss Leader doesn't always step up when they should. "It's extremely demotivating when managers allow bad behavior because they are fearful that it may cause difficulties for them," one employee says of this type of boss.

As with an Unintentional Leader, lack of adequate training or people skills could cause a Hit-or-Miss Leader to be oblivious to how their actions or inactions affect the people around them. Think of Michael Scott, the self-absorbed boss from TV's *The Office* who's friendly until he isn't. They may be checked out during the workday because of family issues or other problems. They may fall short of their own aspirations as a leader as they struggle with extra responsibilities brought on by a merger, a layoff, or keeping up with rapid expansion or change.

Because they often play favorites, intentionally or unintentionally, a Hit-or-Miss Leader may fail to hold people accountable for doing what they're supposed to, or not stand up for people or teams they manage. Likewise, they may not work well with other teams, leading to communication breakdowns. "This can be very frustrating and sometimes it seems like the managers aren't even talking to each other," another employee says of their Hit-or-Miss Leader boss.

As a result, a Hit-or-Miss Leader's effect on the workplace is—you guessed it—hit or miss. Employees who work for this leader type are slightly more inclined to be ambivalent or feel negative about work (53 percent) than feel good about what they do (47 percent). Because Hit-or-Miss Leaders connect with some people more than others, they create an atmosphere of uncertainty, one where people aren't sure they can count on their coworkers. This also leads to a broader erosion of trust, since a climate of doubt among employees is counter to a high-trust culture.

Employees with bosses at this level are 31 percent less likely to say they experience cooperation at work than employees of leaders at the next level, the Transactional Leader. On the other hand, because a Hit-or-Miss Leader creates a less toxic workplace than what people experience under an Unintentional Leader, employees are 36 percent less likely to leave, improving voluntary turnover and with it the bottom line.

If PwC's Tim Ryan had been a Hit-or-Miss Leader, he would never have spoken up about the racial injustices roiling the country. Taking that kind of public stand is the antithesis of a leader who doesn't want to make waves.

You might be a Hit-or-Miss Leader if you...

> Often feel like you're in over your head
> Can't focus due to current problems in your personal life

> Go out to lunch or socialize with the same team members all the time
> Have trouble relating to several people on your team
> Have had direct reports transfer to other departments, complain about you to your boss, or leave for another job
> Have received warnings about not hitting goals or improving your people leadership performance

Leveling Up

A Hit-or-Miss Leader is far from a lost cause. For these bosses to move to the next leadership level they must eliminate favoritism, communicate regularly with people in and outside the teams they manage, keep everyone feeling involved, and routinely show they appreciate people's efforts. If a Hit-or-Miss Leader can do that, the people they work with will gain faith in their integrity and put more effort into their work, which will improve cooperation and productivity.

Level 3: The Transactional Leader

Common employee experience:
"They get the job done—and nothing more."
More than anything, the Transactional Leader values checking things off the list, especially things related to their own goals. They've risen above some negative behaviors associated with Unintentional and Hit-or-Miss Leaders and are good at what they do. But they are mainly concerned with checking tasks off a to-do list or hitting key performance indicators and consequently are not as forward-thinking or charismatic as leaders at higher levels. Though they are heading in the

right direction, a Transactional Leader's style of working and communicating is still inconsistent, and they don't attempt to forge the personal connections necessary for employees to feel empowered and engaged. "A lot of policies and changes come down as management edicts," one employee shared about this type of boss.

A Transactional Leader could be a creature of habit, clinging to old patterns cultivated before digital advances and other innovations that have changed how work gets done and the requirements of the job. They could reflect the way they are treated by their own boss or a bureaucratic organization that doesn't give managers much power. "Middle-level management is unable to set and communicate strategies, and makes decisions accordingly," one employee said.

In the environment a Transactional Leader creates, people take pride in their work and can be counted on to do what they're told. That level of competency also applies to teams they manage, which are good at executing specific, known tasks. Unlike people who work for Unintentional or Hit-or-Miss Leaders, a majority of people (62 percent) with Transactional Leader bosses feel good about their jobs. But because these managers don't always support thinking outside the box, teams are 25 percent less likely to be innovative as those with leaders at the next level up.

Employees working for Transactional Leaders also report more politicking and backstabbing at work than the higher levels, due in part to their boss' nonchalant attitude. They may feel they don't have a voice or don't get enough information about what they are supposed to be doing. "Answers provided by management to date are very vague," one employee says about their Transactional Leader boss. Even though most people with Transactional Leaders are happy at work, 16 percent have a negative experience, and another 22 percent could take it or leave it.

Think back to the example of Marriott in Chapter 5 and the value placed on every employee, regardless of position. A housekeeping associate at a Marriott-owned Ritz-Carlton property described how her supervisors and coworkers supported her after both her parents died. At another organization, working for a Transactional Leader, her experience could have been completely different. Instead of the sympathy she was shown, a by-the-book Transactional Leader wouldn't have wanted to get involved in an employee's personal life. It would have meant doing away with cordial conversations to open up and be authentic. The Marriott associate's bond with the company is no doubt stronger today because of the compassion shown by her boss.

You might be a Transactional Leader if you...

- Value getting things done over talking to people
- Give orders more than you listen to employees' concerns or challenges
- Don't know much about what's going on in people's personal lives
- Feel like a small cog in a bureaucratic machine
- Are recognized more for your technical competency than your soft skills
- Have had direct reports describe you as efficient but cold

Leveling Up

For a Transactional Leader to move to the next level, they have to stop operating on autopilot and start building good people skills and habits. It could mean working to communicate with direct reports more consistently, listening to employees and welcoming their input on decisions, and showing people how their role fits into the big picture. To improve, a Transactional Leader also needs to show their sincere interest in employees as people, so individuals feel like they're being managed in a fair and reliable manner.

Level 4: The Good Leader

Common employee experience:

"I stay because of my manager."

The Good Leader has a distinct edge over leaders at the lower levels. They are consistent, inclusive, and sincere. They are clear about expectations for people's roles, understand that mistakes happen, and realize people have lives outside of work. Employees frequently describe a Good Leader as easy to talk to, understanding, fair, and the reason they stay. For many people, there's very little practical difference between working for a Good Leader and working for a For All Leader. "Immediate management is excellent, and I wouldn't be here if not for them," one person said about this type of boss.

While a Good Leader has a lot going for them, they haven't reached For All Leader status. For all their good qualities, they may feel that the ultimate responsibility for reaching goals lies with them, not their team. Thinking that way may make them less comfortable being open and vulnerable about their own failings, which could prevent them from connecting with some people. A handful of holdouts don't see them as completely competent or reliable communicators. A Good Leader's status as not quite For All is shown in our data. While 80 percent of employees with a Good Leader have a great experience of work, 13 percent are neutral, and 7 percent have a negative experience. Even with a Good Leader boss, people are 25 percent less likely to say they look forward to coming to work than people who report to a For All Leader.

Overall, though, a Good Leader is good for business. Under their watchful eye, employees work well individually and together. People are willing to be flexible, and adopt new skills when the circumstances require it. Employees are 28 percent more likely to give extra than those who work for a Transactional Leader. A company's bottom line benefits from these leaders because fewer employees want to leave. In fact, 13 percent more people say they prefer to stick around for a long time than people who work for Transactional Leaders. They're also good at helping people understand how they fit into an organization and helping them advance in their careers.

Let's look to WP Engine CEO Heather Brunner—a quintessential For All Leader—to illustrate a small yet consequential difference between Level 4 and 5 leaders. As described earlier, Brunner decided to practice open book management, sharing the company's financials and key performance indicators with the entire workforce so they could understand how their jobs fit into the business. If Brunner had been a Good Leader instead of a For All Leader, she might have decided that only managers or sales reps needed to see financials. As a result, the employees left in the dark would be less aware of how different groups work together toward company goals, and unclear how their jobs affect the bottom line.

You might be a Good Leader if you...

> Help employees develop in their careers and recommend them for promotions
> Have been a mentor
> Can talk to anyone on your team about most issues, whether work-related or personal
> Haven't been able to establish a good rapport with a few people whom you just can't seem to warm up to
> Think it's important for others to see you as a leader
> Receive generally good performance reviews, including feedback from peers and direct-reports
> Have been promoted because of your superior management skills

Leveling Up

For a Good Leader to make it to the top, they have to address whatever is stopping them from connecting with the holdouts on their team so everyone feels heard in decisions and feels they can speak up when it matters. To improve, a Good Leader can't just focus on today. They must take the long view and focus both on the future and on how teams across the company fit together to achieve goals. Also, they must be able to articulate an organization's goals in a way that helps people feel inspired and connected to them. Finally, leaders at this level must abandon any ego attached to being the boss, and subsume their own interests in the service of helping others shine.

Level 5: The For All Leader—A Great Leader For All

Common employee experience:

"My manager truly has my best interests in mind."

For All Leaders have a lot to brag about. After all, they've made it to the top of the leadership persona hierarchy, their people love them, and the teams they lead are more successful than teams managed by leaders at other levels.

But here's the thing about For All Leaders: they'd rather leave the bragging to others. If you're familiar with the concept of the servant leader, you'll recognize it in these managers, who prefer to lead from behind, enabling the people who work for them to do their best work. For All Leaders treat all people with dignity, regardless of position. People who work for these leaders see them as hard working and leading by example: they walk the talk. Employees also see them as honest, ethical, and true to their word. One employee describes their manager, who is a For All Leader, as "an amazing, intelligent, transparent, and helpful [leader] who WANTS us to succeed."

For All Leaders aren't micromanagers. They're happy to have people work autonomously, and welcome feedback and others' input on decisions. Showing that they're responsive and open to others increases their own influence. Construction firm TDIndustries, a FORTUNE 100 Best Company to Work For, makes employee empowerment part of its corporate communications mantra: "Everyone participates—no one dominates."

For All Leaders are fair, though fairness in pay and other matters doesn't necessarily equate to treating everyone the same. Fairness also takes into account the socioeconomic systems that historically have favored some people over others and an awareness of how all employees might perceive a leader's actions. At the 100 Best Workplaces, which have an abundance of For All Leaders, employee ratings of fairness have risen more dramatically than any other area in the past 20 years, outpacing advances in respect, credibility, and the other workplace dimensions we study.

The results For All Leaders achieve—or rather, the results their people achieve—are remarkable. Their teams demonstrate productivity that is more than three times higher than those under Unintentional Leaders. Employees led by For All Leaders are also up to three times better at innovating and working at a speedy, agile pace than people who work for leaders at the lowest level. People with For All Leader bosses are also far more likely to want to stay with their companies for a long time.

It's common for employees to say For All Leaders are the best bosses they have ever encountered. For All Leaders make everyone feel welcome and treated fairly and establish a strong sense of collaboration within teams as well as through different areas of the organization. They stand out for their ability to reduce politicking and favoritism to nearly imperceptible levels, perhaps because they do a great job of getting feedback from everyone and involving them in decisions.

For everything they do right, For All Leaders aren't perfect. They are still human, capable of oversights and mistakes. One element that sets them apart from Good Leaders, though, is their ability to inspire loyalty, performance, and growth in others. People who report to For All Leaders often describe doing the best work of their careers. When For All Leaders are at the helm, employees are more inclined to believe that compensation is fair, that colleagues work well together, and that work is an open, friendly, welcoming place. "I can talk about any issues and suggestions with my manager and team members," one employee said.

Again, we can look to WP Engine's Heather Brunner as an example of a For All Leader. Her decisions to remove a college degree requirement from the application process and to train all employees how to read the company's financials stemmed from her conviction that the company would be made stronger with a wide variety of perspectives at the table—and by leveraging the full strength of all their employees' human potential. "One of the things I tell our team is that we're a company of equals," said Brunner. "The only reason that I'm CEO is just time, and different experiences I've had. I'm no smarter, I have no more potential. You have all those things."[149]

You might be a For All Leader if you...

> Surround yourself with smart, engaged people motivated to do their best

> Lead teams that make innovative products and gain above-average business results

> Lead teams that work well with other groups throughout the organization

> Often hear people who report to you say they love their jobs

> Can recall at least a few instances where you have supported a direct report in succeeding but haven't felt the need to take credit for your input

- Have little to no voluntary turnover on teams you manage
- Are frequently asked to be a mentor or have helped multiple people advance in their careers
- Receive positive performance reviews or 360 evaluations
- Have been promoted on the basis of your leadership skills or teams' successes
- Are invited to speak about leadership and what your teams have accomplished, or run workshops on the topic

Remaining a For All Leader

Being a For All Leader isn't easy. Constantly changing business needs, personnel, market conditions, and other demands of the job mean there's no such thing as a status quo. Retaining a For All Leader mindset means constantly reevaluating what people and teams need to be successful—what needs to be done, on the part of the leader, to help the team accomplish their goals. To remain open and flexible, For All Leaders may need to work on their own personal growth, through training, meditation, or other means. It could also take regular reminders of the inherent goodness of the people they are leading, to put problems that come up into perspective.

And regardless of where leaders fall on the spectrum, it's critical to have an accurate understanding of how their teams experience them—for the sake of employees and for the business. If companies are committed to building Great Places to Work For All, all leaders must be guided by accurate data and analytics that give them this understanding. Informed by data, leaders can take targeted action toward continuous improvement.

For All Leaders Move Beyond the Boundaries of Business

Beyond the five personas we've described in this chapter, there is another level to the For All Leader that transcends a single team or even an organization. This is when a person recognizes the power they have to make a bigger difference in the world by using their position as a platform for inspiring change. For inspiring other leaders to become For All Leaders too.

This type of leadership takes a great deal of courage and conviction. In his first week on the job as chairman at PwC, Tim Ryan was advised not to start an honest dialogue about race, but he made the decision to do it anyway, because he knew it was the right thing to do. One could argue that he risked his position of power by doing so. But by turning his position into a platform for large-scale change, he gave voice to the experience of his own employees and inspired many of the country's top leaders to publicly pledge to start the dialogue at their own companies.

Before Beth Brooke-Marciniak, EY global vice chair of public policy, came out as gay, she was strongly advised by some of her closest confidants not to go through with it, given her senior role as a global business leader. But she took the risk because she believed it was more important to use her platform to deliver a strong, positive, and honest message to gay teenagers about what they could achieve. She said that delivering that message was far more important to her than any other consequence. "Much to my surprise," she shared, "I was embraced, and seemingly handed an entirely new platform to make more of a difference than I ever could have imagined."

Ryan and Brooke-Marciniak are examples of business leaders using their platforms to promote positive societal change. A look at the opinions of the FORTUNE 500 CEOs shows this is a role that is only becoming more imperative for top leaders. Just 4 percent of this elite group's 2017 cohort agreed with the statement: "I believe my company should mainly focus on making profits, and not be distracted by social goals." And over half (58 percent) agreed that "as a CEO, it's important to take a stand on some public issues," a number that is steadily rising.[150]

This falls in line with the American workforce's growing belief that business leaders should step up in this way. Public relations firm Weber Shandwick reports that roughly half of millennials believe CEOs "have a responsibility to speak up on issues important to society," as compared to just 28 percent of Gen Xers and baby boomers.[151]

The fact is, being a great leader in the ways we've described is better for business, better for people, and better for the world. You'd be hard-pressed to find a leader who wouldn't want to be named as having the For All leadership traits—and the corresponding teams—that we've described. So you may be asking yourself, why aren't more people For All Leaders?

This is a question we have been asking as well.

Chapter 8
The For All Rocket Ship

Getting to Great Places to Work For All may be hard.
But it's going to be the journey of the twenty-first century.

In this book, we've tried to show leaders that the For All path is viable. That in fact it is desirable.

In the first part, we laid out the business case for Great Places to Work For All. We described the contours of the new economic landscape, where social and technology changes are putting a premium on a human-centric way of doing business. We outlined our new definition of a Great Place to Work For All. We explained why maximizing human potential is central to success today, and how organizations must bring out the best of everyone through values, effective leadership, and trust in order to innovate and grow. We also showed how closing workplace gaps—plugging leaks in your culture—pays off with measurable business benefits like faster revenue growth, increased productivity, and reduced turnover.

We believe the business case is compelling. But it isn't the whole story. So in the second part, we talked about how Great Places to Work For All are better for people and for the world. We detailed how these organizations enable us as individuals to achieve more than we thought possible and to enjoy healthier, more fulfilling lives. And how Great Places to Work For All make for a better global society through greater shared prosperity, fairness, and opportunity.

We followed those high-minded chapters by getting down to brass tacks for leaders. We shared our new research on

10,000 managers and outlined our new For All Leadership Model, painting a picture of leaders at different levels and presenting evidence that providing a great work experience for more of your team members produces better business results.

We also asked this question: who wouldn't want to be a Level 5, For All Leader? We know many are not there yet, even at the best companies. And we wonder why.

Why haven't more leaders taken the steps to build a workplace that is consistently great for everyone, no matter who they are or what they do for the organization? Why haven't more recognized and seized the power of maximizing everyone's potential? Why haven't more learned from 20 years of data pointing to the payoff of high-trust, inclusive cultures? What's more, why haven't more seen a For All workplace as a moral imperative?

Could the resistance to For All lie in the lingering effects of the Industrial Revolution, which sharply divided "brains" from "brawn"? Could it relate to business school teaching that gives short shrift to the people side of organizations and promotes a stingy view of human potential? Might it be that power and privilege are so addictive that they blind us to rational choices that help our businesses?

Could Frederic Laloux be right that our organizations reflect the level of our collective consciousness, with many leaders focused too much on profit and competition? Might biases, such as sexism and racism, be so deeply ingrained that true inclusion will take our species decades or centuries more to achieve?

We think not. In fact, we believe a tipping point is at hand. The Great Workplace movement we helped launch at the end of the twentieth century now has mainstream momentum, and our new For All mission builds on it.

In recent years, for example, many business executives have made a great culture a strategic priority. We have noticed the 100 Best, for their part, getting fairer. We see more and more business leaders rejecting the argument that the pie isn't big enough to give out pieces to all. Instead, they are starting to believe that a For All culture makes the pie bigger so that everyone can have a piece—and the pieces are bigger than in the past!

We see younger people—millennials and our own younger kids—growing up with For All values. Values like appreciating everyone's worth, getting involved, having a voice, and caring about a better world for all human beings.

And shouldn't we be building the world for these young people anyway?

That's why 2030 is a big deal for us. It's the year we expect to have everyone, throughout the entire globe, working at a Great Place to Work For All: a certified Great Place to Work For All—proven by the numbers, by the spring in the step of the people there, by the positive vibe people feel there.

By 2030, we hope the conversations about work will be very different. In 2030, people will look for organizations whose mission and culture are a great fit for them, not just look for ones that are the least boring or stressful or abusive. We hope everybody will look at an organization that they're thinking about joining and see people that look like them, at all levels of the organization. We hope we're not talking about diversity and inclusion in 2030 like we are today—with debates over whether widening the candidate pool to include more women and people of color amounts to "lowering the bar."

We hope that in 2030 all organizations will bring out the best in everyone.

We know this 2030 vision is a bold one. Call it our moonshot.

In fact, we talk about our mission to build a better world through Great Places to Work For All as a rocket ship. We want to get everyone on planet Earth on the For All ship.

It's a new kind of rocket. Consider it a cross between the Saturn rockets that zoomed to the moon and Wonder Woman's invisible jet. On this rocket there will be no more hidden figures. No more people working hard without recognition for their efforts. No more pockets of men or women feeling demeaned or deflated yet obscured by layers of bureaucratic neglect. On this ship—made transparent by data and enlightened leaders—everyone doing their part is seen, acknowledged, and appreciated.

This For All ship will transport us to workplaces that make us feel alive and free and healthy. Workplaces that bring people together across countries and across the globe, advance our prosperity, and elevate our collective consciousness. Workplaces where our leaders find ways to connect with everyone, to develop the full human potential of all.

Will you join the pioneers on the For All Rocket Ship? It takes courage and a willingness to look in the mirror—to truly face up to your beliefs, your values, and your impact as a leader.

And yet the first steps on the journey are simple. There are five:

1. Survey your employees about their work experience.
2. Objectively review what they're saying.
3. Think about how your leadership and the leadership of others needs to change to create an environment where every employee has a better experience regardless of who they are and what they do for the organization.
4. Get help with your leadership practices.
5. Repeat Steps 1–4.

That formula will get you on the For All path—a path that takes you right into the For All rocket.

If you need a final bit of motivation before stepping on board, consider this: it's going to be a fun ride. An adventure into what's possible for human beings as they labor together. Getting to Great Places to Work For All may be hard at times. But it's going to be the journey of the twenty-first century.

Notes

Foreword

1. He told me the name of the bank, which I am not repeating here, but you can try to guess which bank it is.

Introduction

2. John Chambers, interview by Ed Frauenheim and Jessica Rohman, Great Place to Work Conference, Great Place to Work, May 25, 2017.

3. Jay Yarow, "The Greatest Tech Companies in History, Period," *Business Insider*, January 24, 2012, http://www.businessinsider .com/the-greatest-companies-in-the-history-of-technology-period -2012-1; Jena McGregor, "Cisco Names John Chambers's Successor," *Washington Post*, May 4, 2015, https://www.washingtonpost .com/news/on-leadership/wp/2015/05/04/cisco-names-successor -to-longtime-ceo-john-chambers/ (URLs accessed October 10, 2017).

4. John Chambers, interview by Alan Murray, Great Place to Work Conference, Great Place to Work, May 25, 2017.

Chapter 1

5. Chris Ballard, "Steve Kerr's Absence: The True Test of a Leader," *Sports Illustrated*, May 16, 2017, https://www.si.com/ nba/2017/05/16/steve-kerr-nba-playoffs-golden-state-warriors -injury-leadership (accessed October 10, 2017).

6. Scott Ostler, "Warriors united in the poetry of defense," *San Francisco Chronicle*, April 13, 2017, http://www.sfchronicle.com/

sports/ostler/article/Warriors-united-in-the-poetry-of-defense
-11071364.php (accessed November 28, 2017).

7. See Shaun Powell, "Golden State Warriors superstar Kevin Durant moving on from Oklahoma City backlash," *NBA.com,* May 30, 2017, http://www.nba.com/article/2017/05/29/warriors-kevin -durant-moving-thunder-backlash#/ (accessed November 28, 2017); and Marc J. Spears, "'Strength in Numbers' Convinced Kevin Durant to Join Warriors," *The Undefeated,* July 4, 2016, https://the undefeated.com/features/strength-in-numbers-convinced-kevin -durant-to-join-warriors/ (accessed October 10, 2017).

8. Alex Edmans, "The Link Between Job Satisfaction and Firm Value, with Implications for Corporate Social Responsibility," *Academy of Management Perspectives* 26.4 (2012): 1–19.

9. Vivian Hunt, Dennis Layton, and Sara Prince, "Why Diversity Matters," McKinsey & Company, January 2015, http://www .mckinsey.com/business-functions/organization/our-insights/ why-diversity-matters (accessed October 10, 2017).

10. Marcus Noland, Tyler Moran, and Barbara Kotschwar, "Is Gender Diversity Profitable? Evidence from a Global Survey," February 2016, Working Paper No. 16-3, Peterson Institute for International Economics, Washington, D.C., https://piie.com/pub lications/wp/wp16-3.pdf (accessed October 10, 2017).

11. Ed Frauenheim and Sarah Lewis-Kulin, "Pursuing the Potential of All Employees," Great Place to Work, 2016, https:// www.greatplacetowork.com/resources/reports/742-pursuing-the -potential-of-all-employees (accessed October 10, 2017).

12. Louis Columbus, "2015 Gartner CRM Market Share Analysis Shows Salesforce in the Lead, Growing Faster than Market," *Forbes,* May 28, 2016, https://www.forbes.com/sites/louiscolum bus/2016/05/28/2015-gartner-crm-market-share-analysis-shows -salesforce-in-the-lead-growing-faster-than-market/ (accessed October 10, 2017).

13. Anne Shields, "Why Salesforce Is Set to Grow in 2017,"

Market Realist, February 22, 2017, http://marketrealist.com/2017/02
/why-salesforce-is-set-to-grow-in-2017/ (accessed October 10,
2017).

14. Kurt Badenhausen, "The Knicks and Lakers Top the NBA's
Most Valuable Teams 2017," *Forbes,* February 15, 2017, https://www
.forbes.com/sites/kurtbadenhausen/2017/02/15/the-knicks-and
-lakers-head-the-nbas-most-valuable-teams-2017/#ffcdbff7966e
(accessed October 10, 2017).

15. Bruce Schoenfeld, "What Happened When Venture
Capitalists Took Over the Golden State Warriors," *New York Times*,
March 30, 2016, https://www.nytimes.com/2016/04/03/magazine
/what-happened-when-venture-capitalists-took-over-the-golden
-state-warriors.html (accessed October 10, 2017).

Chapter 2

16. Marco della Cava, Jessica Guynn, and Jon Swartz, "Uber's
Kalanick Faces Crisis over 'Baller' Culture," *USA TODAY*, February
24, 2017, https://www.usatoday.com/story/tech/news/2017/02/24/
uber-travis-kalanick-/98328660/ (accessed October 10, 2017).

17. Mike Isaac, "Uber Board Stands by Travis Kalanick as It
Reveals Plans to Repair Its Image," *New York Times*, March 21, 2017,
https://www.nytimes.com/2017/03/21/technology/uber-board
-stands-by-travis-kalanick.html (accessed October 10, 2017).

18. Susan J. Fowler, "Reflecting on One Very, Very Strange
Year at Uber," February 19, 2017, https://www.susanjfowler.com/
blog/2017/2/19/reflecting-on-one-very-strange-year-at-uber (accessed October 10, 2017).

19. Deirdre Bosa and Anita Balakrishnan, "The Justice
Department Is Looking into Whether Uber Violated US Foreign
Bribery Laws, Report Says," CNBC, April 29, 2017, https://www
.cnbc.com/2017/08/29/doj-investigating-whether-uber-violated-us
-foreign-bribery-laws-dj-citing-sources.html (accessed October 24,
2017).

20. Eric Newcomer, "In Video, Uber CEO Argues with Driver over Falling Fares," *Bloomberg*, February 28, 2017, https://www.bloomberg.com/news/articles/2017-02-28/in-video-uber-ceo-argues-with-driver-over-falling-fares (accessed October 10, 2017).

21. Kara Swisher and Johana Bhuiyan, "Uber President Jeff Jones Is Quitting, Citing Differences over 'Beliefs and Approach to Leadership,'" *Vox Media*, March 19, 2017, https://www.recode.net/2017/3/19/14976110/uber-president-jeff-jones-quits (accessed October 10, 2017).

22. Eric Newcomer, "Uber, Lifting Financial Veil, Says Sales Growth Outpaces Losses," *Bloomberg*, April 14, 2017, https://www.bloomberg.com/news/articles/2017-04-14/embattled-uber-reports-strong-sales-growth-as-losses-continue (accessed October 10, 2017).

23. della Cava, Guynn, and Swartz, "Uber's Kalanick Faces Crisis over 'Baller' Culture."

24. Mike Isaac, "Uber Fires 20 amid Investigation into Workplace Culture," *New York Times*, June 6, 2017, https://www.nytimes.com/2017/06/06/technology/uber-fired.html (accessed October 10, 2017).

25. Newcomer, "In Video, Uber CEO Argues with Driver over Falling Fares."

26. Isaac, "Uber Fires 20 amid Investigation into Workplace Culture."

27. Mike Isaac, "Uber Founder Travis Kalanick Resigns as C.E.O.," *New York Times*, June 21, 2017, https://www.nytimes.com/2017/06/21/technology/uber-ceo-travis-kalanick.html (accessed October 10, 2017).

28. John Gerzema and Michael D'Antonio, "The Power of the Post-Recession Consumer," *strategy+business*, February 22, 2011, https://www.strategy-business.com/article/00054 (accessed October 10, 2017).

29. William H. Frey, "Five Charts that Show Why a Post-

White America Is Already Here," *New Republic*, November 21, 2014, https://newrepublic.com/article/120370/five-graphics-show-why -post-white-america-already-here (accessed October 10, 2017).

30. Ibid.

31. Richard Fry, "Millennials Surpass Gen Xers as the Largest Generation in U.S. labor force," Pew Research Center, http:// www.pewresearch.org/fact-tank/2015/05/11/millennials-surpass -gen-xers-as-the-largest-generation-in-u-s-labor-force/ (accessed October 10, 2017).

32. Jonas Barck, "Universum Releases 2017 U.S. Talent Survey Data," *Universum Global,* http://universumglobal.com/ articles/2017/04/universum-releases-2017-u-s-talent-survey-data/ (accessed October 10, 2017).

33. D. Finn and A. Donovan, "PwC's NextGen: A Global Generational Study," PwC, 2013, https://www.pwc.com/gx/en/ hr-management-services/pdf/pwc-nextgen-study-2013.pdf; "Mind the Gaps: The 2015 Deloitte Millennial Survey, Executive Summary," Deloitte, 2015, https://www2.deloitte.com/content/dam/De loitte/global/Documents/About-Deloitte/gx-wef-2015-millennial -survey-executivesummary.pdf (URLs accessed October 10, 2017).

34. Fowler, "Reflecting on One Very, Very Strange Year at Uber."

35. "Social Media Fact Sheet," Pew Research Center, January 1, 2017, http://www.pewinternet.org/fact-sheet/social-media/ (accessed October 10, 2017).

36. Myles Udland, "United Airlines Loses $950 Million in Market Value as Shares Tumble," *Oath Inc.*, April 11, 2017, https:// finance.yahoo.com/news/united-airlines-shares-tumbling-14064 8573.html (accessed October 10, 2017).

37. Derek Thompson, "A World Without Work," *The Atlantic*, July/August 2015, https://www.theatlantic.com/magazine/archive/ 2015/07/world-without-work/395294/ (accessed October 10, 2017).

38. Dov Seidman, "From the Knowledge Economy to the Human Economy," *Harvard Business Review*, November 12, 2014,

https://hbr.org/2014/11/from-the-knowledge-economy-to-the
-human-economy (accessed October 10, 2017).

39. "Hyatt Hotels Corporation's Chief Human Resources Officer, Robert W. K. Webb, YouTube video," 42:47, posted by "Great Place to Work," April 10, 2106, https://youtu.be/uEdlbo FDjzc?t=26m5s (accessed October 10, 2017).

40. Susan Lund, James Manyika, and Jacques Bughin, "Globalization Is Becoming More About Data and Less About Stuff," *Harvard Business Review*, March 14, 2016, https://hbr.org/2016/03/globalization-is-becoming-more-about-data-and-less-about-stuff (accessed October 10, 2017).

41. Vanessa Bates Ramirez, "How to Stay Innovative amid the Fastest Pace of Change in History," Singularity Education Group, May 19, 2017, https://singularityhub.com/2017/05/19/how-to-stay-innovative-amid-the-fastest-pace-of-change-in-history/; Bhaskar Chakravorti, Christopher Tunnard, and Ravi Shankar Chaturvedi, "Where the Digital Economy Is Moving the Fastest," *Harvard Business Review*, February 19, 2015, https://hbr.org/2015/02/where-the-digital-economy-is-moving-the-fastest (URLs accessed October 10, 2017).

42. Lund, Manyika, and Bughin, "Globalization Is Becoming More About Data and Less About Stuff."

43. Ed Frauenheim, "Contingent Workers: Why Companies Must Make Them Feel Valued," *Workforce*, August 3, 2012, http://www.workforce.com/2012/08/03/contingent-workers-why-companies-must-make-them-feel-valued/ (accessed October 10, 2017).

44. Newcomer, "In Video, Uber CEO Argues with Driver over Falling Fares."

Chapter 3

45. A. H. Maslow, "A Theory of Human Motivation," *Psychological Review* 50 (1943): 370–396, http://psychclassics.yorku.ca/Maslow/motivation.htm (accessed October 10, 2017).

46. "fMRI Reveals Reciprocal Inhibition Between Social and Physical Cognitive Domains," *NeuroImage* 66 (2013): 385–401, https://www.ncbi.nlm.nih.gov/pubmed/23110882; "Richard Boyatzis—What Brain Science Is Teaching Us About Leadership," YouTube video, 3:15, posted April 17, 2014, https://www.youtube.com/watch?v=kxR7dNqNbWM (accessed October 10, 2017).

47. Research suggests stereotype threat can harm employees' engagement and organizations' performance, but can be countered through steps such as leaders explicitly affirming inclusivity as a value and feedback in which leaders convey their confidence that the employee can live up to a high standard. See Bettina J. Casad and William J. Bryant, "Addressing Stereotype Threat Is Critical to Diversity and Inclusion in Organizational Psychology," *Frontiers in Psychology*, January 20, 2016, http://journal.frontiersin.org/article/10.3389/fpsyg.2016.00008/ (accessed October 10, 2017).

48. George Serafeim and Claudine Gartenberg, "The Type of Purpose that Makes Companies More Profitable," *Harvard Business Review*, October 21, 2016, https://hbr.org/2016/10/the-type-of-purpose-that-makes-companies-more-profitable (accessed October 10, 2017).

49. Hunt, Layton, and Prince, "Why Diversity Matters."

50. "A Conversation with Randall Stephenson and David Huntley: Code of Business Conduct," AT&T, March 14, 2017, https://ebiznet.sbc.com/attcode/assets/2017StephensonHuntleyVideoTranscript.pdf (accessed November 4, 2017).

51. Juliana Menasce Horowitz and Gretchen Livingston, "How Americans View the Black Lives Matter Movement," Pew Research Center, July 8, 2016, http://www.pewresearch.org/fact-tank/2016/07/08/how-americans-view-the-black-lives-matter-movement/ (accessed November 4, 2017).

52. Luigi Guiso, Paola Sapienza, and Luigi Zingales, "The Value of Corporate Culture," *Journal of Financial Economics* 117 (2015): 60–76.

53. Kim Peters and Ed Frauenheim, "How These Companies Are Changing the Financial Industry," *Fortune,* July 19, 2016, http://fortune.com/2016/07/19/companies-changing-financial -industry/ (accessed October 10, 2017).

54. Ibid.

55. Katherine Schwab, "Ideo Studied Innovation in 100+ Companies—Here's What It Found," Co.Design, March 20, 2017, https://www.fastcodesign.com/3069069/ideo-studied-innova- tion-in-100-companies-heres-what-it-found (accessed October 10, 2017).

56. See Steven C. Currall, Ed Frauenheim, Sara Jansen Perry, and Emily M. Hunter, *Organized Innovation: A Blueprint for Renewing America's Prosperity* (Oxford: Oxford University Press, 2014).

57. Emma Seppala, "Why Compassion Is a Better Manageri- al Tactic than Toughness," *Harvard Business Review,* May 7, 2015, https://hbr.org/2015/05/why-compassion-is-a-better-managerial -tactic-than-toughness (accessed October 10, 2017).

58. Marc J. Spears, "The Mystery Man Behind the Plan that Helped the Warriors Win Game 4 of the NBA Finals," *Yahoo! Sports,* June 12, 2015, https://sports.yahoo.com/news/the-mystery-man -behind-the-plan-that-helped-the-warriors-win-game-4-of-the -nba-finals-080509364.html (accessed October 10, 2017).

59. Steven Ruiz, "Bill Belichick Needed Every Bit of His De- fensive Genius to Beat the Falcons," *USA TODAY,* February 5, 2017, http://ftw.usatoday.com/2017/02/bill-belichick-gameplan-patriots -falcons-super-bowl-51-recap (accessed October 10, 2017).

60. Lund, Manyika, and Bughin, "Globalization Is Becoming More About Data and Less About Stuff."

61. "Sustainable Growth Rate—SGR," *Investopedia,* http:// www.investopedia.com/terms/d/dupontanalysis.asp (accessed October 10, 2017).

Chapter 4

62. Our findings on "gaps" at the Best Workplaces is corroborated by a recent study of Great Place to Work data by scholars Edward Carberry of the University of Massachusetts, Boston, and Joan Meyers of California Polytechnic State University, San Luis Obispo. They studied 1,054 companies that applied for the 100 Best Companies to Work For list between 2006 and 2011 in the United States, and concluded: "the perceptions of men and women of color and white women in companies that make the 'best' list are more positive than their demographic counterparts in companies that do not make the list. We also find, however, that the perceptions of employees from historically marginalized groups are more negative than those of white men in the 'best' workplaces, and these patterns are similar to those in firms that do not make the list. For perceptions of fairness, the differences between employees from historically marginalized groups and white men are smaller in companies that make the list." Edward J. Carberry and Joan S.M. Meyers, "Are the 'best' better for everyone? Demographic variation in employee perceptions of FORTUNE's 'Best Companies to Work For,'" *Equality, Diversity and Inclusion: An International Journal,* Vol. 36 Issue: 7, 2017, pp.647–669, https://doi.org/10.1108/EDI-01-2017-0017 (accessed November 29, 2017).

63. Robert Silverman, "Steve Kerr, the Risk-Taking General Who Led the Warriors to Victory," *Daily Beast,* June 17, 2015, https://www.thedailybeast.com/steve-kerr-the-risk-taking-general -who-led-the-warriors-to-victory (accessed November 29, 2017).

64. Josh Bersin, "Why Diversity and Inclusion Will Be a Top Priority for 2016," *Forbes,* December 6, 2015, https://www.forbes .com/sites/joshbersin/2015/12/06/why-diversity-and-inclusion -will-be-a-top-priority-for-2016/ (accessed October 10, 2017).

65. Gallup has found that 87 percent of employees worldwide are not engaged at work, and that companies with highly engaged

workforces outperform peers by 147 percent in earnings per share. See "The Engaged Workplace," Gallup, 2017, http://www.gallup .com/services/190118/engaged-workplace.aspx. See also Andy Nelson, "Does Employee Engagement Depend on Position Level?" hppy, http://www.gethppy.com/employee-engagement/does -employee-engagement-depend-on-position-level (URLs accessed October 10, 2017).

66. "Inequality Hurts Economic Growth, Finds OECD Research," Organisation for Economic Co-operation and Development, http://www.oecd.org/newsroom/inequality-hurts-economic-growth.htm (accessed October 10, 2017).

67. Bernadette D. Proctor, Jessica L. Semega, and Melissa A. Kollar, "Income and Poverty in the United States: 2015," U.S. Department of Commerce, 2016, https://www.census.gov/library/ publications/2016/demo/p60-256.html (accessed October 10, 2017).

68. Sheryl Sandberg and Adam Grant, "Speaking While Female," *New York Times*, January 12, 2015, https://www.nytimes .com/2015/01/11/opinion/sunday/speaking-while-female.html (accessed October 10, 2017).

69. Susan Chira, "Why Women Aren't C.E.O.s, According to Women Who Almost Were," *New York Times*, July 21, 2017, https:// www.nytimes.com/2017/07/21/sunday-review/women-ceos-glass -ceiling.html (accessed October 10, 2017).

70. Pat Wechsler, "Women-Led Companies Perform Three Times Better than the S&P 500," *Fortune*, March 3, 2015, http:// fortune.com/2015/03/03/women-led-companies-perform-three -times-better-than-the-sp-500/ (accessed October 10, 2017).

71. Cindy Robbins, "2017 Salesforce Equal Pay Assessment Update," Salesforce, April 4, 2017, https://www.salesforce.com/ blog/2017/04/salesforce-equal-pay-assessment-update.html (accessed October 10, 2017).

72. Louis Columbus, "2015 Gartner CRM Market Share

Analysis Shows Salesforce in the Lead, Growing Faster than Market," *Forbes*, May 28, 2016, https://www.forbes.com/sites/louiscolumbus/2016/05/28/2015-gartner-crm-market-share-analysis-shows-salesforce-in-the-lead-growing-faster-than-market/ (accessed October 10, 2017); Shields, "Why Salesforce Is Set to Grow in 2017."

73. Ed Frauenheim and Shawn Murphy, "Caring as Competitive Weapon," Great Place to Work, January 13, 2017, https://www.greatplacetowork.com/blog/787-caring-as-competitive-weapon (accessed October 10, 2017).

74. See, for example, David Rock and Heidi Grant, "Why Diverse Teams Are Smarter," *Harvard Business Review*, November 4, 2016, https://hbr.org/2016/11/why-diverse-teams-are-smarter (accessed October 10, 2017).

75. "Report: Pursuing the Potential of All Employees," Great Place to Work, December 5, 2016, https://www.greatplacetowork.com/resources/reports/742-pursuing-the-potential-of-all-employees (accessed October 10, 2017).

76. "Job Fulfilment, Not Pay, Retains Generation Y Talent," iOpener Institute, 2012, https://iopenerinstitute.com/wp-content/uploads/2016/04/iOpener-Institute-Gen-Y-Report.pdf (accessed October 10, 2017).

77. "7 Ways High-Trust Organizations Retain Talent," Great Place to Work, February 3, 2016, https://www.greatplacetowork.com/reports/626-2016-100-best-companies-to-work-for (accessed October 10, 2017).

78. "How Millennials Want to Work and Live," Gallup, http://www.gallup.com/reports/189830/millennials-work-live.aspx (accessed October 10, 2017).

Chapter 5

79. Employee comments from 2017 Great Place to Work–Certified companies.

80. "Employee Engagement in U.S. Stagnant in 2015," Gallup, January 13, 2016, http://www.gallup.com/poll/188144/employee -engagement-stagnant-2015.aspx (accessed October 10, 2017).

81. Jim Clifton, "The World's Broken Workplace," LinkedIn Corporation, June 13, 2017, https://www.linkedin.com/pulse/ worlds-broken-workplace-jim-clifton (accessed October 10, 2017).

82. Studs Terkel, *Working: People Talk About What They Do All Day and How They Feel About What They Do* (New York: New Press, 1974).

83. Seidman, "From the Knowledge Economy to the Human Economy."

84. *Merriam-Webster*, s.v. "respect," https://www.merriam -webster.com/dictionary/respect (accessed October 10, 2017).

85. Online Etymology Dictionary, s.v. "respect," http://www .etymonline.com/index.php?term=respect (accessed October 10, 2017).

86. Arne Sorenson, Marriott, Fireside Chat with Matt Heimer, 2017 Great Place to Work Conference, May 25, 2017.

87. Employee comments from 2017 Great Place to Work– Certified companies.

88. Steve Taylor, "Slighting: The Dangers of Being Disrespect-ed," *Psychology Today*, January 22, 2017, https://www.psychology today.com/blog/out-the-darkness/201201/slighting-the-dangers -being-disrespected (accessed October 10, 2017).

89. Kai Cao and Sanqing Wu, "Abusive Supervision and Work-Family Conflict: The Mediating Role of Emotional Exhaus-tion," *Journal of Human Resource and Sustainability Studies* 3 (2015): 171–178, http://file.scirp.org/pdf/JHRSS_2015120214580440.pdf (accessed October 10, 2017).

90. Christine Porath, "Half of Employees Don't Feel Respect-ed by Their Bosses," *Harvard Business Review*, November 19, 2014, https://hbr.org/2014/11/half-of-employees-dont-feel-respected -by-their-bosses (accessed October 10, 2017).

91. Great Place to Work, 2016 100 Best Workplaces for Women analysis.

92. Gillian B. White, "The Alarming, Long-Term Consequences of Workplace Stress," *The Atlantic*, February 12, 2015, https://www.theatlantic.com/business/archive/2015/02/the-alarming-long-term-consequences-of-workplace-stress/385397/ (accessed October 10, 2017).

93. Paul J. Zak, "The Neuroscience of Trust," *Harvard Business Review*, January–February 2017, https://hbr.org/2017/01/the-neuroscience-of-trust (accessed October 10, 2017).

94. Great Place to Work, FORTUNE 2017 100 Best Companies to Work For in America, Trust Index Survey Results.

95. "2015 Training Industry Report," *Training*, https://trainingmag.com/trgmag-article/2015-training-industry-report (accessed October 10, 2017). While *Training* magazine's report found an overall increase in training spending in 2015, large companies on average cut training budgets that year.

96. Josh Bersin, "The Corporate Training Market Is Exploding," Deloitte Development, January 30, 2013, http://blog.bersin.com/the-corporate-training-market-is-exploding/ (accessed October 10, 2017). Bersin by Deloitte's study of the training market found significant dips in training spending during the recession years of 2008 and 2009, though training spending has increased in recent years.

97. Ronald J. Burke, *The Fulfilling Workplace: The Organization's Role in Achieving Individual and Organizational Health* (London: Routledge, 2013), Ch. 3.

98. Mark DeWolf, "12 Stats About Working Women," U.S. Department of Labor, March 1, 2017, https://blog.dol.gov/2017/03/01/12-stats-about-working-women; "Introducing the 2017 Fortune 500 List," *Fortune* video, 1:52, http://fortune.com/fortune500/ (URLs accessed October 10, 2017).

99. Sylvia Ann Hewlett, Laura Sherbin, et al., "Athena Factor

2.0: Accelerating Female Talent in Science, Engineering and Technology," Center for Talent Innovation, 2014, http://www .talentinnovation.org/assets/Athena-2-ExecSummFINAL-CTI.pdf (accessed October 10, 2017).

100. "GoDaddy Joins Fair Pay Pledge to Help Close the Gender Pay Gap," *Cision PR Newswire,* June 14, 2016, http://www .prnewswire.com/news-releases/godaddy-joins-fair-pay-pledge-to -help-close-the-gender-pay-gap-300284629.html (accessed October 10, 2017).

101. Auguste Goldman and Monica Bailey, Go Daddy, "Driving Unconscious Bias Out of Our Culture," presentation, 2017 Great Place to Work Conference, May 24, 2017.

102. "The State of Entry-Level Employment in the U.S.," March 2017, the Rockefeller Foundation and Edelman Intelligence, https://assets.rockefellerfoundation.org/app/uploads/2017 0320171306/Impact-Hiring-Survey-Results.pdf; T. Ross, T. Kena, A. Rathburn, A. KewalRamani, J. Zhang, P. Kristapovich, and E. Manning, "Higher Education: Gaps in Access and Persistence Study," National Center for Education Statistics, August 2012, https: //nces.ed.gov/pubs2012/2012046.pdf (URLs accessed October 10, 2017).

103. Heather Brunner, WP Engine, "Starting at the Core: Building an Engaged and Transparent Culture," presentation, 2017 Great Place to Work Conference, May 24, 2017.

104. Charles Duhigg, "What Google Learned from Its Quest to Build the Perfect Team," *New York Times,* February 25, 2016, https://www.nytimes.com/2016/02/28/magazine/what-google -learned-from-its-quest-to-build-the-perfect-team.html (accessed October 10, 2017).

105. Shannon B. Wanless, "The Role of Psychological Safety in Human Development," *Research in Human Development* 13 (2016): 6–14, https://www.researchgate.net/publication/296623430_The

_Role_of_Psychological_Safety_in_Human_Development (accessed October 10, 2017).

106. Beth Brooke-Marciniak, EY, "GPTW4ALL Leadership Story," keynote presentation, 2017 Great Place to Work Conference, May 24, 2017.

107. Tim Ryan, PwC, Fireside Chat with Alan Murray, 2017 Great Place to Work Conference, May 24, 2017.

108. Nancy Vitale, Genentech, "GPTW4ALL Leaders Panel: Navigating the Complexities of '4ALL' in a Global Business," with Ellen McGirt, 2017 Great Place to Work Conference, May 24, 2017.

109. Ellen McGirt, "175 CEOs Join Forces for Diversity and Inclusion," *Fortune,* June 12, 2017, http://fortune.com/2017/06/12/175-ceos-join-forces-for-diversity-and-inclusion/ (accessed October 10, 2017).

110. Dan Ariely, Emir Kamenica, and Drzen Prelec, "Man's Search for Meaning: The Case of Legos," *Journal of Economic Behavior & Organization* 67 (2008): 671–677, http://faculty.chicagobooth.edu/emir.kamenica/documents/meaning.pdf (accessed October 10, 2017).

111. "7 Ways High-Trust Organizations Retain Talent," Great Place to Work.

112. Great Place to Work, 2016 Culture Audit from W. L. Gore & Associates.

113. Great Place to Work, 2016 Culture Audit from Recreational Equipment, Inc.

Chapter 6

114. Margot Lee Shetterly, *Hidden Figures* (New York: HarperCollins, 2016), p. 190.

115. See Calla Cofield, "NASA's Female Leaders Share Challenges of Working in Male-Dominated Field," Space.com, March 21, 2016, https://www.space.com/32317-nasa-female-leaders-womens-history-month.html (accessed October 10, 2017).

116. See Richard Paul and Steven Moss, *We Could Not Fail: The First African Americans in the Space Program* (Austin: University of Texas, 2015), p, 121.

117. Bob Granath, "NASA Helped Kick-start Diversity in Employment Opportunities," National Aeronautics and Space Administration, July 1, 2016, https://www.nasa.gov/feature/nasa-helped-kick-start-diversity-in-employment-opportunities (accessed October 10, 2017).

118. "2017 Edelman Trust Barometer," http://www.edelman.com/trust2017/ (accessed October 10, 2017).

119. Steven Radelet, *The Great Surge: The Ascent of the Developing World* (New York: Simon & Schuster, 2015); Louis Uchitelle, *The Disposable American: Layoffs and Their Consequences* (New York: Knopf, 2006).

120. "Chart Book: The Legacy of the Great Recession," Center on Budget and Policy Priorities, August 8, 2017, http://www.cbpp.org/research/economy/chart-book-the-legacy-of-the-great-recession (accessed October 10, 2017).

121. "Americans' Financial Security," Pew Charitable Trusts, March 2015, http://www.pewtrusts.org/~/media/assets/2015/02/fsm-poll-results-issue-brief_artfinal_v3.pdf (accessed October 10, 2017).

122. Workplace accidents that lead to injury and death are not a major concern for most U.S. workers. But in other parts of the world—especially in less-wealthy countries—physical safety on the job remains a real issue. See International Labour Organization, "Safety and Health at Work: Hopes and Challenges in Development Cooperation," 2013, http://www.ilo.org/safework/projects/WCMS_215307/lang--en/ (accessed October 10, 2017).

123. White, "The Alarming, Long-Term Consequences of Workplace Stress."

124. Shana Lynch, "Why Your Workplace Might Be Killing You," *Insights by Stanford Business*, February 23, 2015, https://www

.gsb.stanford.edu/insights/why-your-workplace-might-be-killing
-you (accessed October 19, 2017).

125. Eliza Mackintosh, "Report: Income Inequality Rising in
Most Developed Countries," *Washington Post*, May 16, 2013, https://
www.washingtonpost.com/news/worldviews/wp/2013/05/16/
report-income-inequality-rising-in-most-developed-countries/
(accessed October 10, 2017).

126. Richard Wilkinson, "Why Inequality Is Bad for You—
and Everyone Else," CNN, November 6, 2011, http://www.cnn
.com/2011/11/06/opinion/wilkinson-inequality-harm/ (accessed
October 10, 2017).

127. "Inequality Hurts Economic Growth, Finds OECD
Research," Organisation for Economic Co-operation and Development.

128. Jim Clifton, "What the Whole World Wants," Gallup, December 17, 2015, http://www.gallup.com/opinion/chairman/187676
/whole-world-wants.aspx (accessed October 10, 2017).

129. Clifton, "The World's Broken Workplace."

130. "Deloitte Announces 16 Weeks of Fully Paid Family Leave
Time for Caregiving," Deloitte, September 8, 2016, https://www2
.deloitte.com/us/en/pages/about-deloitte/articles/press-releases/
deloitte-announces-sixteen-weeks-of-fully-paid-family-leave-time
-for-caregiving.html (accessed October 10, 2017).

131. Kerry Jones, "The Most Desirable Employee Benefits,"
Harvard Business Review, February 15, 2017, https://hbr.org/2017
/02/the-most-desirable-employee-benefits (accessed October 10,
2017).

132. "2017 PEOPLE's Companies That Care," Great Place to
Work, 2017, https://www.greatplacetowork.com/best-workplaces/
companies-that-care/2017 (accessed October 10, 2017).

133. Robert Levering, "This Year's Best Employers Have
Focused on Fairness," *Fortune*, March 2, 2016, http://fortune.com

/2016/03/03/best-companies-2016-intro/ (accessed October 10, 2017).

134. "The Great Workplace Era Emerges in Asia," Great Place to Work, 2015, https://s3.amazonaws.com/bestworkplacesdb/publications/The_Great_Workplace_Era_Emerges_in_Asia.pdf (accessed October 10, 2017).

135. Stephen Knack, "Trust, Associational Life and Economic Performance," paper prepared for the HRDC-OECD International Symposium on the Contribution of Investment in Human and Social Capital to Sustained Economic Growth and Well-Being, http://www.oecd.org/innovation/research/1825662.pdf (accessed October 10, 2017).

136. Kenneth Arrow, "Gifts and Exchanges," *Philosophy and Public Affairs* 1 (1972): 343–362, cited in http://www.oecd.org/innovation/research/1825662.pdf (accessed October 10, 2017).

137. "Chapter 3: Inequality and Economic Mobility," Pew Research Center, May 23, 2013, http://www.pewglobal.org/2013/05/23/chapter-3-inequality-and-economic-mobility/ (accessed October 10, 2017).

138. "2017 Edelman Trust Barometer."

139. Frederic Laloux, *Reinventing Organizations* (Brussels: Nelson Parker, 2014), p. 44.

140. Robert Wright, *Nonzero: The Logic of Human Destiny* (New York: Pantheon Books, 2000).

141. Margot Lee Shetterly, *Hidden Figures* (New York: Harper-Collins, 2016), p. 248.

Chapter 7

142. "Mayvenn, Inc.," Great Place to Work, 2017, http://reviews.greatplacetowork.com/mayvenn-inc; "About Us," Mayvenn, 2017, https://shop.mayvenn.com/about-us (URLs accessed October 10, 2017).

143. "GoFundMe," Great Place to Work, 2017, http://reviews.greatplacetowork.com/gofundme (accessed October 10, 2017).

144. Jun Loayza, "With $2 Billion Raised, GoFundMe Wants to 'Disrupt Giving' by Putting Philanthropy in Our Hands," Startup Grind, https://www.startupgrind.com/blog/with-2-billion-raised-gofundme-wants-to-disrupt-giving-by-putting-philanthropy-in-our-hands/ (accessed October 10, 2017).

145. "United States Small Business Profile," U.S. Small Business Administration Office of Advocacy, 2016, https://www.sba.gov/sites/default/files/advocacy/United_States.pdf (accessed October 10, 2017).

146. Frauenheim and Murphy, "Caring as Competitive Weapon."

147. Clifton, "The World's Broken Workplace."

148. Employee comments from 2015 to 2017 Trust Index Surveys.

149. Heather Brunner, WP Engine, "Starting at the Core: Building an Engaged and Transparent Culture."

150. Alan Murray, "CEO Daily: Tuesday, 6th June," *Fortune*, June 6, 2017, http://fortune.com/2017/06/06/ceo-daily-tuesda-6th-june/ (accessed October 10, 2017).

151. Alan Murray, "Trump Veers Off-Script, Again," *Fortune*, August 6, 2017, http://fortune.com/2017/08/16/trump-veers-off-script-again/ (accessed October 10, 2017).

Thanks

This book is an important part of our mission to build a better world by helping organizations become Great Places to Work For All, and we'd like to recognize everyone who helped to create it.

Steve Piersanti and the team at Berrett-Koehler Publishers, thank you for your steadfast enthusiasm and support of For All, and for helping us change the world by reaching people around the globe with this message.

Tabitha Russell, Nancy Cesena, Chandni Kazi, and our friends at Datable, including Daniel Gibson, Matt Lichti, and Lull Mengesha: thank you for your impeccable analysis of the vast amount of data that helped form the themes of the book. Without your efforts we'd have inspiring words alone. Your data points will help move the needle toward real change.

Thank you to our amazing design partners at Majorminor for your work on the cover design and graphic elements of the book. Thank you to Carolyn Monaco, Jill Totenberg, and Melissa Kranz for your experienced insights in helping our For All message reach the public, to Tessa Herns for helping to manage the book's marketing and distribution, and to Cecilia Riva Mosquera for your efforts to bring the book to an international audience.

We'd also like to thank Lizelle Festejo and Jamie Holt for coordinating the Great Place to Work For All conference, which brought hundreds of people together to publicly discuss the For All message and led to many of the insights featured in this book.

Thanks also to everyone who provided writing and editing support: Michelle Rafter for your editorial assistance in preparing the manuscript, and Teresa Iafolla, Casey Li, Tyler Matheny, and Kristen McCammon for additional editing and research support.

We'd like to recognize and thank the many inspiring leaders featured in this book, who have set a high bar for leaders everywhere as they work toward For All: Monica Bailey, Auguste Goldman, and Blake Irving of GoDaddy, Beth Brooke-Marciniak of EY, Heather Brunner of WP Engine, John Chambers of Cisco, Tim Ryan of PwC, Arne Sorenson of Marriott International, Randall Stephenson of AT&T, and Nancy Vitale of Genentech.

To all of our colleagues at Great Place to Work in the U.S. and around the world, thank you for your unwavering commitment to our mission. This work is possible only through our shared belief that a better world can—and will—be achieved through our collective efforts.

We also want to tip our hat to our cofounder and prior owner Robert Levering, to our other cofounder and pivotal leader Amy Lyman, and to the visionary Reuben Ly for making magic happen.

Our ownership change in 2015 and the resulting board leadership has made our recent technology and analytics advancements possible. These innovations have enabled the development of our new methodology and our Accelerated Leadership Performance product. For that we thank our new owners, Katharine Whalen, Dan Whalen (chairman of the board), Melba Wu, and Michael Bush.

Finally, we'd like to thank the many companies and leaders who work tirelessly to build Great Places to Work For All, and the millions of employees who work there. You are our inspiration. The dedication, sweat, conviction, humanity, and creativity at the best of these companies bring out the best of us here at Great Place to Work, and give us a hopeful vision of what the world can be.

Index

The letter *n* following a page number denotes an endnote, and the letter *f* denotes a figure.

About Us

Great Place to Work is the global authority on high-trust, high-performance workplace cultures, with offices in more than 50 countries. Our mission is to build a better world by helping organizations become Great Places to Work For All. Over the last 30 years, we have performed in-depth research centering on the employee experience of what makes an organization great and have now defined the pinnacle For All workplace. Decades of research show workplaces with high-trust cultures see higher returns to the bottom line, levels of innovation, customer and patient satisfaction, employee engagement, and organizational agility.

Our clients benefit from an unparalleled set of benchmarking data and best practices from leading companies around the world along with an industry-proven research methodology. Each year, as many as 4 million employees globally at more than 6,000 companies take our Trust Index Employee Survey—firms that collectively employ roughly 10 million people. The companies we survey represent virtually every size and every industry.

Through our Certification Programs, Great Place to Work publicly recognizes outstanding workplace cultures and produces the annual FORTUNE 100 Best Companies to Work For list—now for over 20 years—and Best Workplaces lists for millennials, women, diversity, small and medium companies, and various industries. We also partner with premier business publications around the world to produce international Best Workplaces lists in 58 countries across six continents.

Through our tech-enabled global consulting services, we help our clients create great workplaces that outpace peers on key business metrics like revenue growth, profitability, retention, and stock performance. Building a high-trust, high-performance culture for all employees is a journey, and we at Great Place to Work know the path for all sizes of organizations to navigate. Utilizing our proprietary emprising SaaS platform, we offer a thoughtful, data-driven, and systematic approach, designed to accelerate change among leaders and across the entire organization.

We practice what we preach on the inside of Great Place to Work. We're business-minded people at a mission-driven company, and we are a Great Place to Work ourselves. We know what it takes because we live it.

Follow Great Place to Work at greatplacetowork.com and @GPTW_US.

Accelerating to For All with Great Place to Work Products and Services

More than ever, today's leaders must be guided by accurate data and analytics as they make strategic culture change. Informed by data-driven insights, leaders can achieve the results they want for their workplace with maximum efficiency, leaving little to chance or misinterpretation.

Consulting

Great Place to Work offers tech-enabled global consulting services that help our clients create great workplaces that accelerate business performance. This includes our High-Trust Culture Consulting Services and the Accelerated Leadership Performance offering.

Accelerated Leadership Performance (ALP) uses the AI in our emprising platform to produce the prescriptive data to show leaders how they stack up as a Level 5 For All Leader. The ALP assesses the employee experience of their leader and of the workplace overall, and provides each leader with personalized scores, recommended focus areas, and custom, concrete prescriptions so they can accelerate improvement in the employee experience and business performance of their unique team. Figure 21 illustrates the kind of improvement we forecast within a single organization whose managers use the ALP. Each manager is given one or two key recommendations their survey data shows would drive the greatest level of change for their team. Over time, leaders can move the needle more quickly in their employees' experience and in their teams' business results.

Certification

Through our Certification Program, companies of all sizes have the opportunity to be publicly recognized as Great Place to Work–Certified and to earn a spot on the many lists we produce in the U.S. and around the world. Our Certification Program also allows companies to quantify their culture with our Trust Index Employee Survey, to benchmark their employees'

Figure 21

Accelerate Leadership Performance to Be Great For All

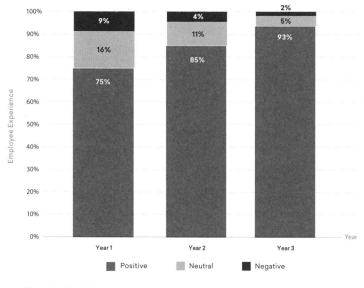

Source: Great Place to Work analysis

experience against the very best, and to use these insights to improve their workplace and their business results.

For more information about our Certification Program, visit https://www.greatplacetowork.com/certification.

Authors

Michael C. Bush is CEO of Great Place to Work, where he leads the global enterprise of more than 50 offices around the world. Under Michael's leadership, Great Place to Work has evolved its mission and methodology to recognize companies that build great workplaces for all employees, regardless of who they are or what they do for their company. Before joining Great Place to Work in 2015, he served as president of the 8 Factors, an online learning organization that he founded; CEO of Clark Sustainable Resource Developments; and CEO of Tetra Tech Communications, which he grew from $40 million to $300 million in revenues. Michael is a founding board member of the private equity seed-fund, Fund Good Jobs, which educates, accelerates, and invests in small inner-city businesses that lead to equitable communities for all. Michael has taught entrepreneurship courses at Stanford University and Mills College, and served as a member of President Obama's White House Business Council. He earned his M.S. in management from Stanford's Graduate School of Business. Michael lives in his hometown of Oakland, California, with his wife Melba. Michael has two adult sons, Matthew and Martin, and a daughter in-law Lisa, married to Matthew. He can often be found playing jazz saxophone with his septet "The Ways and Means Committee" in the Bay Area.

Ed Frauenheim is director of research and content at Great Place to Work. He authors research reports, conducts data analysis, and produces commentaries related to great workplaces in the United States and throughout the world. He codeveloped Great Place to Work's Trust Mindset concept and has led several workshops on the topic. Before coming to Great Place to Work in 2014, Ed spent 15 years as a journalist and commentator focused on the intersection of work, technology, and business strategy. He has published articles in outlets including FORTUNE, *Wired,* and the *Seattle Times*, spoken at numerous events, and cowritten two books: *Organized Innovation: A Blueprint for Renewing America's Prosperity* and *Good Company: Business Success in the Worthiness Era*. Ed has a bachelor's degree in history from Princeton University and a master's degree in education from the University of California at Berkeley. Ed lives in San Francisco with his wife, Rowena, and two kids, Julius and Skyla. In his spare time you can find him cheering for the Warriors, playing basketball himself, and dancing to Daft Punk.

ANDRIA LO

Jessica Rohman is director of content at Great Place to Work and leads the development of content furthering Great Place to Work thought leadership. Jessica spent many years of her career as an organizational development consultant, working with leaders across industries to help improve the employee experience. She also led the Executive Strategy Network, a professional network for leaders of recognized 100 Best Companies. Since she began working at Great Place to Work in 2004, she has conducted extensive research on many of the best workplaces in the world, and has been featured as an expert on great workplaces for media outlets such as the *Miami Herald*, *Diversity Woman* magazine, and Oprah.com. She is also a frequent contributor to FORTUNE magazine. Jessica holds a B.A. in psychology and an M.A. in industrial and organizational psychology. She has also conducted doctoral studies in human and organizational systems at the Fielding Institute. Jessica lives in Berkeley, California, with her husband, Kris, and two children, Charlotte and Blake.

JUSTIN COIT

Sarah Lewis-Kulin is vice president of certification and list production at Great Place to Work. She is a frequent contributor to FORTUNE magazine with articles on research related to best companies. She developed Great Place to Work's standard for certifying organizations as great workplaces. She also spearheaded the creation of Great Place to Work's new For All methodology, which assesses the degree to which a company creates a consistently positive experience for employees, regardless of who they are or what they do for the organization. Sarah continues to oversee the evolving analysis determining Great Place to Work's many Best Workplaces lists in the U.S., including the FORTUNE 100 Best Companies to Work For. Since joining Great Place to Work in 2000, she has consulted with clients, started the organization's conference and networking programs, and served on its management team. Previously she worked in nonprofits and publishing. She graduated from Wellesley and lives in Massachusetts with her wife and sons.

ANDRIA LO

Ann Nadeau currently serves as the chief people officer and chief marketing officer at Great Place to Work. Ann leads the global brand strategy to build brand awareness and connection while supporting organizational change through rapid organizational growth. In her previous roles as global managing director and vice president of international operations, Ann led the team that provided marketing, business development, product, training, and operations management for 50 countries worldwide. She expanded Great Place to Work's business and mission into more than 30 new countries by launching Best Workplaces list partnerships, creating a successful intellectual property licensing model, and launching the first-ever Best Workplaces lists in Europe and Latin America.

Prior to Ann's current roles at Great Place to Work, she served as head of brand marketing for California-based Joie de Vivre Hospitality, leading the introduction of the Joie de Vivre brand and opening of more than 15 unique hotel and restaurant brands. She earned a B.A. from the University of Michigan and M.S.B.A. from San Francisco State University. Ann lives in Oakland, California, with her wife, and together they co-own two acclaimed restaurants.

ANDRIA LO

Marcus Erb loves using data to better understand the world and make it a better place. As he says himself, he's been extremely fortunate to have been doing exactly that at Great Place to Work for 15 years and counting. In his current position, he leads GPTW's Innovation and Development team, which focuses on developing the next set of tools and insights to help companies build better workplaces for their people and performance. In his previous experience, Marcus worked for an international research and management consulting firm specializing in customized customer satisfaction, performance measurement, strategic development, and organizational assessment programs. Marcus received his B.A. in psychology from Occidental College in Los Angeles and his M.S. in analytics from Villanova University. In his free time, you will likely find him enjoying the beautiful outdoors of the San Francisco Bay Area, rooting loudly for the Giants and Warriors, and laughing trying to keep up with his two young daughters.

Berrett–Koehler
Publishers

Connecting people and ideas
to create a world that works for all

Dear Reader,

Thank you for picking up this book and joining our worldwide community of Berrett-Koehler readers. We share ideas that bring positive change into people's lives, organizations, and society.

To welcome you, we'd like to offer you a free e-book. You can pick from among twelve of our bestselling books by entering the promotional code **BKP92E** here: http://www.bkconnection.com/welcome.

When you claim your free e-book, we'll also send you a copy of our e-newsletter, the *BK Communiqué*. Although you're free to unsubscribe, there are many benefits to sticking around. In every issue of our newsletter you'll find

- A free e-book
- Tips from famous authors
- Discounts on spotlight titles
- Hilarious insider publishing news
- A chance to win a prize for answering a riddle

Best of all, our readers tell us, "Your newsletter is the only one I actually read." So claim your gift today, and please stay in touch!

Sincerely,

Charlotte Ashlock
Steward of the BK Website

Questions? Comments? Contact me at bkcommunity@bkpub.com.

MIX
Paper from
responsible sources
FSC® C016245

Certified

Corporation
bcorporation.net

Berrett–Koehler
Publishers

Berrett-Koehler is an independent publisher dedicated to an ambitious mission: *Connecting people and ideas to create a world that works for all.*

We believe that the solutions to the world's problems will come from all of us, working at all levels: in our organizations, in our society, and in our own lives. Our BK Business books help people make their organizations more humane, democratic, diverse, and effective (we don't think there's any contradiction there). Our BK Currents books offer pathways to creating a more just, equitable, and sustainable society. Our BK Life books help people create positive change in their lives and align their personal practices with their aspirations for a better world.

All of our books are designed to bring people seeking positive change together around the ideas that empower them to see and shape the world in a new way.

And we strive to practice what we preach. At the core of our approach is Stewardship, a deep sense of responsibility to administer the company for the benefit of all of our stakeholder groups including authors, customers, employees, investors, service providers, and the communities and environment around us. Everything we do is built around this and our other key values of quality, partnership, inclusion, and sustainability.

This is why we are both a B-Corporation and a California Benefit Corporation—a certification and a for-profit legal status that require us to adhere to the highest standards for corporate, social, and environmental performance.

We are grateful to our readers, authors, and other friends of the company who consider themselves to be part of the BK Community. We hope that you, too, will join us in our mission.

A BK Business Book

We hope you enjoy this BK Business book. BK Business books pioneer new leadership and management practices and socially responsible approaches to business. They are designed to provide you with groundbreaking and practical tools to transform your work and organizations while upholding the triple bottom line of people, planet, and profits. High-five!

To find out more, visit **www.bkconnection.com**.